Past Tense

CHARLIE'S STORY

Don
Enjoy !
Charlie Hobbs.

C H A R L I E   H O B B S

Published by

GENERAL STORE
PUBLISHING HOUSE

1 Main Street Burnstown, Ontario, Canada K0J 1G0
Telephone (613) 432-7697 or 1-800-465-6072

Layout and cover design by Robert Hoselton

General Store Publishing House Inc. gratefully acknowledges the assistance of the Ontario Arts Council and the Canada Council.

Canadian Cataloguing in Publication Data

Hobbs, Charles, 1920–
    Past tense — Charlie's story

ISBN 1-896182-11-9

        1. Hobbs, Charles, 1920– . 2. Air pilots, Military—Canada—Biography.
3. World War, 1939–1945—Personal narratives, Canadian.   4. Canada, Royal
Canadian Air Force—Biography.   I. Title

D811.H63 1994   940.54´4971´092   C94-900830-3

First Printing 1994

Dedicated

to my son, Gordon,

for his assistance in preparing this book

and to the men I flew with

in World War II

Table of Contents

- CHAPTER 1 -

Charlie's Story

Following the First World War, it was still popular to have babies and, in 1920, my father was advised that in the coming year he would again be presented with a blessed event. True to form, I came along, blue booties and all.

That was in North Bay, where Dad was working as a relief manager of a national bank. Since terminology changes over the years, I will mention that this did not mean he was on relief. Although, as he told me many years later, on his pay it did seem like it.

Dad was a First World War vet who had been very badly wounded at Paschendale. By diligent exercising he had regained use of his leg. He walked every day of his life and wore out many a pet dog in his eighty-odd years.

My mother was a World War I war bride and a nursing sister in the Royal Infirmary in Glasgow when she met my father. After the refinements of growing up in Edinburgh, she must have been jolted by some of the living conditions she experienced during my father's many transfers throughout the province.

Dad had no formal education, except public school, but was very well spoken and well read. As I said, he walked every day. A banker, he wore a stiff white collar attached to his shirt, a well knotted tie and a suit. When he left our home near Broadview Avenue, in Toronto, and headed west, he must have stood out a

1

little. Some of these streets were pretty rough. You wouldn't dare do that today, but he never had any problem and seemed to have more understanding of human nature and the so-called working man than anyone I've ever known. In recalling all this, it is easy for me to know how I loved him so much.

A boy who is still one of my closest friends today was in my first class and every class I attended at Jarvis Collegiate. John Slatter and I seemed to hit it off because of mutual interests ... sports and girls. We had become a part of a group of young people that spent a great deal of time together.

In the summer we would double date and invite girls to *"open air"* dancing at Sunnyside. The dance floor was cordoned off and marble floored. The Sea Breeze, as it was called, was a very romantic place for us with a full-sized orchestra and a price of ten cents a dance to fit our budget with very little to spare. Few of us were going steady and since, in those days, the boys paid the shot, it gave us the prerogative of changing the dates regularly.

One of my favourite dates was John's sister, Mary, who was just one year behind him at Jarvis. She was a good dancer, which helped me to stay on my feet. She was a very popular girl, and her school chums made up half of our group of girlfriends and escorts. John often invited us up to their large family cottage at Jackson's Point on Lake Simcoe, and we had the use of his father's car. His father was also a banker but, more importantly to me, a man who suffered greatly from wounds from the First World War. I had the greatest respect for him and enjoyed his company. He was a most gracious host.

My sister, Evelyn, had completed her schooling by now and been accepted for nursing at Sick Children's Hospital, in residence and in training. She loved her work, but it was exhausting. When she got home on the odd weekend, we would talk for hours. She would tell me about the visitors and about her little patients that she loved so dearly. My own life was shared mostly by people of my own Anglo-Saxon background, but hers was downtown where the beginnings of an ethnic mix were becoming apparent as Toronto began to grow.

In 1938, both John Slatter and I were looking for jobs so that when school ended we could get to work. When the Dominion

2

Charles, Margo, Evelyn
and Harold Hobbs. 1938

Evelyn

Bank asked for a letter of recommendation, John Slatter's father supplied me with one. He also worked for the Dominion Bank, which didn't hurt at all. I was hired at four hundred dollars a year, plus one hundred dollars cost-of-living allowances for the city.

My father, who worked for the Bank of Commerce, supplied John with a similar letter, and he was taken on staff by the Commerce. All of this rigamarole had to do with a ruling at that time that no two members of one family could be hired.

I was now a junior clerk bringing home eighteen dollars every two weeks, less pension deductions. If only I could get a fifty dollar raise, Dad would no longer need to subsidize my income to pay my car fare! But alas, this was a whole year away.

My first bank branch was at Queen and Jamieson in Parkdale. This was a lovely district in those days and the merchants along Queen seemed to be hanging on despite the Depression. As a junior, I had to deliver bank drafts for acceptance. This was a common way of payment, and it acted as a legal receipt for merchandise received, as well as a document to guarantee payment to the manufacturer. A junior also picked up drafts that had been left for signature, and the odd girlfriend.

In a small branch the junior clerk also ran the savings ledger. This kept me pretty busy between ten and three daily but, on balance days, I worked until I balanced every penny, no matter how late it was. With experience, I also learned the current ledger.

Having become such a knowledgable young fellow by now, the bank transferred me to the Bloor and Bathurst branch, again on savings ledger, but with no more drafts to service since they had a full time messenger. He was a man of fifty but was still called a messenger. There were two female employees, and at least I figured this was a step in the right direction. It was a much bigger branch. A point of interest here, though; women at the time were not allowed on permanent staff. Therefore, they could not get on the bank pension plan. One employee, Aggie, had been here for over twenty years and knew every position, but was entitled to no pension.

At the previous branch, the manager had stressed the importance of taking the "Bank Course" and now I was hearing it again from the new manager. The course cost two hundred dollars, which you got back if you passed. My year's pay of five hundred dollars less two hundred left me with three hundred dollars, out of which the bank withdrew my retirement pension. My friends then threw in the last straw, "Well, at least you're working!"

About the same time, Britain declared war on Germany and, within a week, Canada joined Britain. From then on, the whole ball game changed. As thousands of other young men did, I joined up and signed on as Aircrew in the Royal Canadian Air Force. Aircrew was a voluntary service, but the waiting list was so long that I would not be called up until 1940.

When the war started, the Air Force consisted of just a few men and a few aircraft. They needed thousands of men and aircraft, living quarters and airdromes. This was a colossal task. Anyone joining as a tradesman was taken on immediately, but Aircrew required training after all the other work had been completed, and so we waited.

One of Canada's commitments to the war was the task of training Aircrew from all the British Empire countries. New uniforms were beginning to appear from all around the globe, including the British Isles, and our girls were being propositioned in all sorts of languages and dialects. As well, many foreign volunteers were swarming in from Norway, Poland, Holland, several South American countries, and the United States.

On the job I was still being pressured to take the bank course, but I now had the perfect excuse: "I'm waiting to be called up any day now." I referred to this at home as my two hundred dollar excuse! Two of my fellow workers had also signed up for the Air Force and were also waiting, with their two hundred dollars still intact.

The newspapers were beginning to fill up with advertisements for war workers at much improved wages. The war had certainly stirred up the economy.

It would be the best part of a year before I was called up by the Air Force and, once I had committed myself, I began to get impatient. There was nothing I could do about it but sit and wait, carrying on with my job at the bank and fending off the "bank course" as best I could. The manager sure did have a nasty scowl.

- CHAPTER 2 -

Joining Up

Reporting to 55 York Street for Aircrew medicals was rather harrowing. Why, they even showed me where the wild goose goes — but the one-legged balancing tests were tougher. Finally, the colour blind tests and the night flying tests were conducted. There was no sliding scale on the colour tests. You either passed or failed. If you failed, you were given the option of either release or transfer to some other branch of the R.C.A.F. We were told it took ten men to back up one aircraft crew flyer, so lots of jobs were available.

When the tests and interviews were completed, my application was marked "P or O" and I was advised that I would be called. I had qualified as a pilot or observer. An observer was a combination navigator/bomb aimer, or so I was told.

The trip from 55 York Street to Manning Depot did not qualify for either flying time or danger pay so, when next they called me to pick up my orders, they advised me that I was now on the pay-roll. I had to lower my expectations and use a street car.

My new high class accommodation was quite familiar to me. I had been assigned an upper bunk in the horse palace. Often in my teen years, I had been in this building for the Toronto Exhibition and the Royal Winter Fair. We were at the Manning Depot for about thirty days while we were indoctrinated, vaccinated, medicated and directed. Thousands of men were wandering around these buildings with a dazed look, as they tried to absorb what was required of them. Dozens of men, usually the biggest ones, would pass out when their turn came up for shots or needles. There would be one hundred men ahead of them in three lineups, which gave them plenty of time to get scared. They then marched us and fed us.

We were confined to barracks for a week or so until these jobs were done, but we could use the canteen. Until then I didn't drink, but I was about to learn, although I was only eighteen and the legal age was twenty-one. All that changes in uniform. "If you're old enough to fight, you're old enough to drink."

I didn't really need a drink, but I went along with my new friends. Dozens of ladies were working in the canteen — all volunteers, all appreciated. Old sergeants saved by the war were back in uniform and accepting all the free drinks in the world from the new recruits who looked in awe at the stripes. One fresh recruit didn't show respect and was met by a cold stare and comment from the sergeant as he pointed to his stripes. "What do you think them are? Rhubarb?"

Lots of girls showed up at the canteen for dancing and I met one that I thought was mighty cute and asked her for a date. My chum did the same and we both took the street car to where my girl lived. The other girl had agreed to meet us there. Bitsy hinted that she didn't mind a little you-know-what. I wasn't dead certain what she meant by this, but my expectations were high and my curiosity was whetted.

Her father came in to the living room while we where there. He had a big boozy smile on his face and addressed his daughter, "Oh Air Force eh - be sure you wear your tin pants."

"I will," said the daughter.

"Well, make sure he doesn't have a can opener."

All of this helped me to understand why a plumber gets paid so highly, I'm sure.

We didn't see much of our bunk mates during the day. They were probably in a different part of the service. Every possible trade was represented there.

I learned fast to protect my wallet. Thefts were common and some of the thieves were quite bold. One used a sharp knife to remove a money belt from an airman while he slept. The penalty for this was severe, as I soon learned when a thief was caught red handed. A big crowd gathered, then the Military Service Police turned their back on the thief and let the airmen take over. I'm surprised he survived. Jail and dishonourable discharge were minor punishments compared to the broken bones.

About fifty of us designated for Aircrew became a "course" and were given a number which accompanied us all the way through our training at Toronto. We went on marches in Toronto and often we were taken by transport to the ranges at Long Branch to learn how to hold a rifle. Farm boys were quite at home with firearms and needed little training. The same thing applied to driving, although many of us had little or no experience.

Outfitting had not been too difficult for the fitter because he just didn't take it very seriously. He told me I was more or less a standard size ... mostly less. The sleeves fit, except they were six inches too long! My first forty-eight hour pass was coming up, so I took all of my alterations with me. I felt fortunate that my home was in Toronto because the pants I was wearing had legs folded right back up to my knees.

When I got home I did a quick inventory of my friends and found that out of fifteen boys in my class in Jarvis, seven had signed on for the Air Force. Duncan Sinclair, Bill Gunn, Lou Parker, John Slatter, Bill Thomas and Doug Appleton were among these. As was indicative of Toronto in those days, nearly all were Anglo-Saxon.

It was beginning to dawn on me that I knew nothing about flying and might not recognize an aircraft when I saw one. By keeping my mouth shut and my ears open I did learn that the front end of an aircraft was called the nose.

While waiting for your own course to be shipped out to one of the Initial Training Schools, you were sent "somewhere" to do guard duty. When you asked for Calgary, Alberta, you got Summerside, Prince Edward Island, and so on. Fifteen members of our course were sent to Chatham, New Brunswick, via St. Hubert for further outfitting, then for a short stint at Picton, Ontario for guard duty, rifle and all. It was nearly Christmas and I was still nineteen.

Picton had two things wrong with it at that time. The winter of 1940 was very severe and the snow was very deep. This airport, which was soon to be taken over by the Royal Air Force, sat on high ground where the wind took a vicious swipe at us. Standing outside these hangers on guard duty gave me genuine concern for the state of my youthful equipment.

That week we had a visit from a messing officer from Headquarters in Ottawa, following through on a complaint about conditions in our kitchen and mess hall. He arrived unannounced and went directly to the mess hall at meal time. He joined the line up and received his meal. He took one look at the mess he was offered and that's where the fun began.

He heaved his plate against the wall where it hit with a good bit of noise. He then asked for the civilian chef and fired him and all of the hired help on the spot. By this time, cheers were coming from every direction. The officer then thanked those responsible for contacting his office and said he might need a few volunteers for a few days to fill in. That was the first time I ever saw anyone volunteer for K.P.!

Ten days later we were in Montreal overnight and billeted in a Bell Telephone Depot in Westmount. The military police who guarded the depot told us we were not to leave the premises and to close the windows after we left.

Fifteen of us left to find a night club with a floor show. One of the boys won a jitterbug contest and was presented with a large bottle of wine. Free bottles of beer began to arrive from all over the hall and the party was on. Girls appeared from all directions, adding to the enjoyment and confusion. I won't say we won their hearts, but we sure loosened their purse strings.

By four in the morning, the military police were killing themselves with laughter at the futile attempts of some of the gang trying to climb in the windows of the Bell Telephone Depot. They finally ended up helping us. Quite a night!

We were met the next morning by our driver — not a very popular move, but a necessary one. We were to go to St. Hubert to a huge supply depot for winter outfitting. At present, we did have regular uniforms and overcoats, but no other winter supplies such as heavy underwear, sweaters, scarves or hats. The warehouse that served as a supply depot must surely have been sealed up since the First World War. There were bales and bales of fur caps made of beaver skins and moccasin type flying boots, as well as the regular type. These, I believed, were still used by the Royal Canadian Mounted Police at northern outposts. Imagine the out-cry today! Above all, there were snow boots, which I had never seen before. They were made entirely from felt padding about a half inch thick. They were light, handsome, and the most comfortable shoes I had ever worn. Where we were going we were going to need them.

From there we boarded a train headed for Moncton and from there it was on to Chatham, New Brunswick.

Our three month stay at Chatham was unique — we were sent to guard an airdrome which had not yet been built. We were billeted in private homes and went out to the airport site each day by an Air Force van and driver which had been assigned to us. The cook house was already built, and the guard house was complete with plumbing and two rooms for sleeping. They were now working on the first "H" hut, which we would move into when finished. In the meantime, we were quite happy boarding in town. "Town" was where the girls lived, and I must admit we were well treated. The airport was ten miles out of town, with huge snow banks every mile of the way, and certainly not an attractive alternative.

On the second day, an officer arrived from Moncton to advise us that our sergeant in charge would be arriving momentarily along with his corporal, and we would from now on receive our instructions through them. This sergeant's name was St-Germain, the corporal's name I have forgotten and since our flying officer promptly returned to Moncton, where he remained for three months, he probably left his name — but not with me.

St-Germain laid on a two-hours-on, four-hours-off schedule for us around the clock for the front gate. Your turn came up every fourth day but, if it was after dark, you slept. You see, there was nothing else to guard. Although there was some talk among our men about total exhaustion, I think it had more to do with the trips to town than guard duty.

Our Commanding Officer seemed to understand that if they

left us alone we would leave them alone, and that's just the way it was. When in need of greater diversion than our guard duties provided us, we paid the Moncton transport drivers fifty cents each for driving us into town and we arranged return transportation via the barbershop as a pick-up point.

In April, we were moved back to Victoriaville, Quebec. Our new home was in an abandoned monastery. This wooden structure was huge. There was a church, or a large chapel, surrounded by a lot of rooms. On the second and third floors, if I remember correctly, were about fifty plain rooms suitable for monks or trainees.

An important daily duty was a shift known as a fire picket. The old part of the building would have been gone in minutes if anyone had been foolish enough to smoke there and leave a live butt behind. There were two gallon pails placed every ten yards in every corridor and on every floor. To do picket duty on the third floor was quite an ordeal. There was no electricity there so we used a flashlight. Every time we passed one of those cave like rooms, which would be in total darkness until dawn, shivers went up our spines.

To form our class at I.T.S., our group from Chatham was joined by about fifty other men who had been doing their guard duty at other bases across Canada. There were plenty of new faces, some from foreign lands. One Texan in particular, Charlie Rice, stands out in my mind. He was everything I pictured a Texan to be. Shoulder length golden hair, sideburns, cowboy hat and dungarees. A really handsome cuss! When we went on parade, Charlie was spotted immediately and verbally raked over the coals. The officer told the warrant officer to have Charlie escorted to the barber shop for a real hair cut. But Charlie was only one of at least twenty men charged with dress infractions — mostly shoes and, thinking back, I'm not surprised. We had hardly seen dress shoes for three months. We wore felt shoes under galoshes because of the thick snow at Chatham.

When Charlie returned to parade square the next day, I didn't even recognize him. All of his golden locks were shorn off and a winter service hat sat on top. I have made extensive enquiries as to what the name of these hats was. Each time, the reply was "a piss pot." Now, I already knew it was called a piss pot but, in

12

Royal Canadian Air Force

This is to Certify that,

Flying Officer   C. E. McCobbs

has been awarded a Bar to the Operational Wings of the Royal Canadian Air Force, in that he has completed a second tour of operational duty, in action against the enemy.

Dated this   Tenth   day of January 1946

Robert Leckie

ROYAL CANADIAN AIR FORCE
HEADQUARTERS, OTTAWA.

AIR MARSHAL
CHIEF OF THE AIR STAFF.

deference to more delicate ears, I tried to find the correct name. Fearing that if I phoned headquarters for this information, they would put me on charge for describing it as being like a piss pot, I decided to just refer to it as a piss pot.

The Air Force had, of course, built a one storey school with staff offices as well as more dormitories. This was Initial Training School (I.T.S.) Number Fifteen. We drilled hard here and studied even harder, since this was the school that decided if we could fly in Aircrew and what trade we could be in if we passed. Eventually I would be accepted as either pilot or observer. The other categories were airgunner, wireless airgunner or flight engineer. Either way, we had six weeks of exceptionally hard work ahead.

We wrote tests after the lectures and put in a lot of home-work. Some of this stuff was heavy going. Mathematics played a big part in our studies. They stressed the fact that the mechanics of flying was only a part of our future work and gave us a course in basic radio transmission and Morse Code, both sending and receiving. No ten words a minute, no pass! We then took a beginner's course in armaments and took our first Browning Machine gun apart and reassembled it (tough, tough, tough!), learned how to set up the sights on these guns, and took a very elementary course in aircraft recognition. We had a solid six weeks of this before exams. Although most of us passed, we were relieved to get the word.

When a forty-eight hour pass was due, a chum and I decided to hitch-hike to Sherbrooke, a much larger town than Victoriaville. We did so with some difficulty. We were picked up by an army car which, I guess, was illegal. The young soldier told us that his officer had ordered him to pick up some supplies in Sherbrooke and get back as soon as possible. He got one thing right. Nobody but nobody rode in the front seat with the drivers. This suited us just fine and we sat back fully relaxed in the back seat until we noticed his high speed and the fact that he was wandering. A minute later, he bounced off the side of a bridge that we were crossing and, just after crossing, came to a fast stop in a ditch at the side of the road. Neither Joe nor I were hurt and, other than bruises, the driver said that he was okay.

The driver then pleaded with us to leave him since we just

compounded his problems. That suited us just fine. There was something wrong here though — we were leaving the scene of an accident. Joe and I decided to phone our station and leave a message that if an accident was reported, we might be able to help. We returned after our leave and, sure enough, we were called off parade to talk to an army captain and an air force officer. The Captain told us that the driver of an army automobile had an accident on the road from Victoriaville to Sherbrooke and needed help to find two Air Force men to confirm that he had not allowed them to sit up front with him when they were hitch-hiking. We confirmed this, there were no other questions, and we were thanked and dismissed. The Air Force officer contacted us later to advise that he was a lawyer and was present to prevent self-incrimination on our part. For us that was the end of it, thank goodness.

It was now the end of May 1941.

- CHAPTER 3 -

Time to Fly

Our first opportunity to fly would be coming up soon now and, within days, notification of transfer would come through. Half my course was going to Sky Harbour at Goderich, Ontario. The civilian flying school at this drome had contracted with the Air Force to give us elementary flying training. They flew Fleet Finches, which were bi-plane, single engine craft with a huge radial motor up front and seated two, one behind the other. You see, I already knew there was more to a plane than the nose ... clever, eh?

Our time was divided between school classes and flying. My first flight was both exciting and frightening. I wondered how anything made of fabric could stay up in the air. By the time a month had passed, I had grown to love flying. When we progressed to aerobatics and learned to do a roll, I found I could do this — providing I remembered to open my eyes in time to prevent a second roll. Then we did a loop by bringing the nose up the stick, tight to our tummy. You were soon upside down and having some second thoughts, but sooner or later you came over, down and up to your former height. Then you asked, "Where the Hell am I?"

One of our classmate's "Daisy Mae" backed into a prop one day, and he was killed instantly. At thirty-three years of age, Doug had been the oldest member of the Commonwealth Training team, a man who was so very capable that everyone looked up to him. He had been a top fastball player at the Beaches in Toronto and at Goderich, playing twice a week for the local town team. He helped all of us when he could, including taking very good care of a six foot, two inch bully on our course. We felt his loss keenly. We were just not prepared yet for the heavy loss of friends we would witness overseas.

The most famous name on this course was Hornell, who later received the Victoria Cross for his submarine attacks in the North Sea, but at that time was just a pleasant unassuming friend. His story is one of pure heroism.

It took me a while to solo and I made one serious mistake. Just before my solo, I was checked out by the chief instructor, a very heavy man. All of our landings were made without power, so we just glided in to our huge grassy airfield. I approached correctly, flying into the wind, came over the trees and had just cut the motor when the sheer weight of my passenger cut my glide down to a straight flat, three point drop, leaving me with my two wheels on the airfield and the little rear wheel in the ditch. Furthermore, I had knocked the wind out of the very man who had the power to pass or fail me. He did not speak a word while I gunned the motor. To make things worse, once out of the ditch, he had to climb back in because we were still a mile from the tarmac straight ahead. I felt like taking off again! We seemed to taxi forever, but finally got there. Such a decent man; he couldn't speak yet, but he did not fail me.

Twice, while at Goderich, we went to Wonderland Pavilion in London for outdoor dancing, the same place where Guy Lombardo got his start. It was a lovely setting for that time of the year, with lots of good looking girls!

Reports from the battlefronts were not the best these days and the R.A.F. were not having their own way either. Since a quarter of the R.A.F. were Canadians, our own casualties were rising, the demand for Aircrews was constant and many more training schools were opening in Canada. Large numbers of my school mates and fellow bank mates were ending up in the Air Force. In addition to the Canadians serving in the R.A.F., we also had more and more of our own Canadian Squadrons serving in England.

The ground school part of Elementary Flying School was difficult and called for careful studying. Mechanical workings, including engines, were completely new to many of us city boys from the high schools, although the Technical School graduates had studied these subjects intensively. To have driven a car was also an asset. Half the graduates would go to single engine training as future fighter pilots and the other half to twin-engine aircraft as Bomber pilots or Transport or Ferry Command pilots.

Once again, we were waiting for the results of exams and our flying tests, and then we would be moving on. I did pass and went on to Brantford Number Five Service Flying School for twin-engine training. At Brantford, they flew Ansons, which were considered a fairly stable aircraft. The other half of our Sky Harbour course was sent to Borden for Service Flying on Harvards and would eventually go to Britain for further training on fighters or as instructors in Canada.

When we left Victoriaville two months before, we had been issued with white flashes to wear in our forage caps. These added a sporty look to the uniform and designated "Aircrew in Training." Now was a time to show this off at home, since we had a three day leave coming up. Upon our return, we would report directly to Brantford.

Once at Brantford, I would be less than sixty miles from home. To hitch-hike was the only way to go. The public really had the spirit now and just about everyone would stop to give a service man a ride or a meal or an introduction to his neighbour's wife.

I found Mom and Dad were doing okay. Evelyn, however, was still nursing but not feeling too well. Evidently, a doctor's check-up could not reveal anything wrong. She was an R.N. now and I was very proud of her. She was still working at Sick Children's Hospital, as well respected then as it is today.

Dad had only about four years to go before retirement, and they were looking forward to moving to the country because both Mom and Dad loved their garden. Besides, all his walking had just about worn out the pavement in Toronto and it was time to move out. His house lease had a couple of years to go, but a Toronto By-law had just been passed which effectively froze rents.

I believe this came under The War Time Prices and Trade Ruling and may have been federally enforced. I made little effort to go out to the West End, but did some phoning to keep track of my chums who were mostly still in training in Canada. Unfortunately for me, the girls already had their Saturday night dates lined up, if they hadn't married since the last time I saw them.

Our half of the course was now settled in Brantford awaiting instructions and, again, a large part of each day would be at ground school learning navigation, map reading, motors and the theory of flight. In the air, we all had a lot to learn. You didn't intentionally throw an Anson into a roll or spin as you did with the Fleet Finch! Co-ordinating the twin engines into a smooth flight was important. I never did get the feeling that I was controlling the aircraft and I don't think I was a very good twin-engine pilot, but I carried on until a week before graduation. Blind flying was also tough for me, but it was an accident that caused my demise, an accident right on the tarmac in front of the tower where the two Ansons collided and, by careful planning, I was able to chew the wing off the other aircraft. It was promptly suggested that, seeing as I was so destructive, I might like to be an airgunner.

This suggestion was more like an order, so I was given my boarding pass for Trenton where all the other re-musters were handled. Due to the accident, I needed clearance from both the Doctor and the Dentist at Brantford. Mac Heatherington and I drowned our sorrows that evening. He had been a good friend all the way through, and Mac continued to do well in the Air Force.

The next morning, the Doctor looked a bit concerned about my condition but, when I explained the reasons, he went along and signed my release.

That afternoon I was on my way to Trenton. I had over one hundred hours of solo flying behind me, which would never do me any harm, but my immediate plans would need clarification. The following morning I had interviews to assess my future, as I now had three options for staying in Aircrew. The first option was as Observer, which was a combination of navigator and bomb aimer; the second was as Wireless Operator; the third was as

Gunner, which would mean up to another six months of courses. However, before I had to make my decision, we were advised of an immediate need for airgunners to take a crash course and be on our way overseas within six weeks. This offer was open to volunteers only and I decided to take it.

True to their word, about sixty of us were bussed to Mountainview Bombing and Gunnery School, just south of Belleville on the highway to Picton and less than twenty miles from Trenton. School would start in forty-eight hours. Trenton had been so overcrowded they had bunked us on cots in a sea-plane hangar. When the big doors were rolled open in the mornings, the fog swept in. Mountainview was also on the Bay of Quinte. It sat high above the water on a sort of plateau. To look down from an aircraft here was a beautiful sight, with water visible on every side.

Trenton was a permanent force station. Mountainview also acted as an emergency landing strip and, due to the length of the runways, could handle very big planes. For our airgunnery, we used Fairy Battles and air cooled machine-guns. Most of the pilots were Polish, and they sure lived up to their wild reputations. The local girls may not have understood their language, but they understood their intentions. To watch them operate at the local dances was a sight to behold. Since this seemed to be the national pastime, we were in there often.

Once again, we had a lot to learn and only six weeks to do it in. Unfortunately, we did not have turrets available. We relied entirely on a relatively simple mechanism called a Vickers. Once this was mastered, we started air-to-ground and air-to-air firing. When we took off, each student was allotted two drums of shells. A drum sat on top of the gun and rotated like a wheel. Half the three-zero-three cartridges were tracers, so that you could follow the flight of your shells. The target Flyers used the naughtiest language, especially if your shells were creeping too close to them or cut the rope between them and the canvas "drogue," or target. Some of them were so experienced, they would carry on for five minutes and never use the same swear word twice. This steady flow was enough to make some of the boys forget that this was their first flight in an aircraft.

There were two gunners in the back of the aircraft, one sitting below and one standing at the open position at the rear. Since the glycol flames were thick in a battle, you were better standing at the gun than down under. Range six hundred yards, effective range three hundred yards and please don't shoot down the drogue pilot!

The course did finish on time and they needed gunners so badly that the only men who failed were those who could not master air sickness. This should have set the alarm bells in my head ringing. No one had told us the job was dangerous before, but you see now what volunteering can do! I remember our first day at Manning Pool when the corporal asked if anyone could swing a prop and all volunteers were handed a mop.

My mother and sister came to Mountainview for Wings Parade and, with a great sense of pride, I received my Gunner's Wing. However, none of the guys seemed to pay attention to the ceremony — they were all staring at my twenty-one year old sister. It was a nice day and, following the reception, my room mates escorted my sister, as a forethought, and my mother, as an afterthought, to the train station where, without realizing it, they put them on the express train to Montreal. I guess no one ever thought there would be two trains out of Belleville in one day, and within fifteen minutes of each other. They did, however, correct this just in time and transferred them to a Toronto train.

There were ten names on the graduation list eligible for commissions, and there were only two commissions for sixty-four men. Both of these commissions went to Americans. The next mouthful will be a little hard to swallow, but here we go: One of those two had just been released from an Alabama chain gang and, within nine weeks, he had been appointed an officer in the R.C.A.F! His name was George Harsh and he wrote a book about it.

- CHAPTER 4 -

Preparing for Overseas

We were granted an "embarkation leave," which meant that all our papers were to be forwarded to us at home, or elsewhere, if we requested. Our return destination was Y Depot, Halifax. We knew we would be going overseas, but exactly where, we didn't know. Autumn would be approaching soon; a nice time of year for two weeks leave. 1941 had been a busy year.

I was concerned about telling Mom that I would be leaving soon, but she accepted it very graciously. I knew Dad would understand, since he had been through it all before. I didn't know what to expect of the future, but there was an excitement building inside me.

Johnny Slatter was home for a few days, so we each found a date. Johnny's sister, Mary, had just become engaged so she was out, but another girl from my school days, Mae Goodall, was available and Johnny got hold of Ruth Janney. I can't for the life of me remember where we went, but we had good company so it didn't matter.

Jack Alexander was a Radar Technician with the R.C.A.F. and he was leaving soon for England. Hudson Mossop, from the East End, was an electrical artificer in the Navy and was stationed in Halifax. He was a good friend and I would look him up soon. Armour Weir, from my class at Jarvis Collegiate, had also joined the Navy. Bill Gunn, Bill Thomas and Lou Parker were Air Force.

I guess those in my age group were just ripe for all of this! My chums from school days were no longer congregating at Robertson's. Many of them went on to university and would join the Officers' Training there. When you took this direction, you completed your university and were then obligated to serve in uniform until the cessation of hostilities. A lot of people felt this was a dodge to avoid service.

It was during this leave that Evelyn was hospitalized at Sick Children's Hospital and they could not seem to pin down the source of the problem. It was so difficult for me to sit in a chair across the room from her, with a nurse on duty, when all I wanted to do was run over and hug her. We had been close friends all our lives, but the nurse would not allow me to approach her. It was a terrible time to tell her I was leaving for overseas. Although she seemed to recover for a while, this was the last time I saw her alive.

The next morning I took the street car along Bloor to Bathurst and visited my last Bank Branch. I am pleased to report that no one asked me to take the bank course. I spoke to the Manager and the Accountant and advised them of my forthcoming move. Things in the branches would be changing quickly now and there would no longer be an over-supply of help available. I was still on staff, but considered to be on leave-without-pay. The bank would pay my pension dues, however. Now, how could they afford that on my salary?

My farewell for Halifax would be coming up in a couple of days and I had promised to meet some of the Toronto boys that were going with me. The lower floor of the Royal York was the usual meeting place in those days, and no invitation was needed. If you were Air Force and passing through Toronto, that was the spot to be. There was something permanent about the old pub there and not much chance of missing anyone since the pubs were open for restricted hours only.

Finally, it was time to say goodbye to Mom and to assure her that it would be a long time before I would see any action. As it turned out, it was over six months. Dad came with me to the train station which, of course, was alive with uniforms in those days. Charlie Rice was standing there waiting. He had completed his pilot's course and was heading to Y Depot. His language was neither English nor Texan, but it was colourful! Later Dad mentioned this to me and I had to explain that the Air Force was not based on a local recruitment where you were with old neighbours in the same regiment, but was made up of men from all over the world and from all walks of life.

The trip would probably take two days and there were no sleepers for us, even with our new sergeant stripes, so we kept our kit bags handy. It was early September, 1941, and the weather was beautiful. I watched out the window as all the familiar names went by: Whitby, Oshawa, Bowmanville. Two hours later we passed Trenton and Belleville, where we had trained, and then on to Kingston where the Ottawa passengers changed. We were now half-way to Montreal. I realized what a vast country this was.

Overnight on a troop train was a long night. Kit bags and airmen were everywhere and the Army gave us a friendly raspberry when they stumbled through the coach past the poker players and over the craps blankets, which the railway supplied for a more civilized purpose. The army was promptly told where to go, of course, but nobody took this advice and, besides, it would be too uncomfortable.

Quebec City was next, then the long run across New Brunswick for the new day and on into Nova Scotia. We arrived in Halifax late and tired. Y Depot sat high on the hill in Halifax and near to the Citadel, a world landmark. You could see across the harbour where there were hundreds of ships of all sizes and shapes, but none of the huge passenger liners that could take five thousand men at one crack. They were never still.

We went back to the stores again where they issued us with battledress and slacks. This less formal attire was very comfortable and would be worn everywhere unless full uniform was mandatory.

Hudson Mossop was handy when I called and he invited me over to the Navy Yards. He was an electrical artificer working with torpedoes, and he showed me a number of items that were new to me and gave me a rough idea of how torpedoes worked. We had lunch together and I went back to Y Depot after a very pleasant day. I did not see Hudson again until after the war.

Some of us spent an evening or two downtown just walking around the old city — and I mean old. Sometimes this was a block or two of "sailors' town," where crews from all over the world congregated. I don't think there was a rougher place anywhere. The constantly busy shore patrols were both American and Canadian which, in itself, surprised me. Jeeps, patrol wagons and big white billets, just bouncing, made quite a sight.

There was nothing for us to do now but wait for the next convoy to be assembled. We were not yet confined to quarters but warned, on threat of court martial, not to leave Halifax. Tough talk; tough enough to keep us near the barracks. A warning was posted that we were now in a war zone and I'm sure this hadn't dawned on us before.

- CHAPTER 5 -

My Twenty-First Birthday

My twenty-first birthday would be overseas after all. We had little warning when the word came down and, within two hours, our kit bags were packed and we were on our bus headed to the dockside. Two hundred passengers came on board and all went into staterooms with two per room. This was a sixteen thousand ton cargo ship with only one deck of passengers. Believe me, we lived very well! We had both room stewards and dining room stewards. The meals were terrific. But, there was a problem. The ship didn't leave dockside for two days and nearly all the men were seasick. I am pleased to report that my luck held, but not without some help. My room mate, Jimmy Jaycks from Toronto, didn't drink so I headed for the nearly empty bar. Although I hadn't yet been seasick like so many others, I felt it was just a matter of time. The bartender suggested I try a Tom Collins but, at my age, I wasn't up on fancy drinks. My fast and furious drinking education had been on beer and whisky, so I took his word for it and my tummy settled right down after I tried his long gin and soda. Since this turned out to be a long crossing, I hoped and prayed that they would not run out of soda.

The S.S. Akaroa carried cargo from New Zealand and Australia to Britain on a regular run. Since she was big enough to carry armament, our airgunners manned the gun positions on the bridge. Each side had an Oerlikon machine-gun mount and an ammunition supply in a metal box. These positions were just as exposed as a rear turret. There was a railing around you, but there was also an awful lot of water about fifty feet below. We worked two hour shifts during daylight hours and wrapped up warmly. The crew brought us oilskins and seemed to appreciate what we were doing. As the barrels were in terrible shape, we asked if the engine crew could let us have some oil rags. We gave the barrels a good pull through and then dry oiled the working parts. We finished off by placing condoms over the barrels to protect them from salt spray. We now had the Merchant Marine's first AIDS-free machine guns. Ah! If the world had only listened.

There was also a four pounder midship, but this was the job of the armament officer who, on a merchantman, was probably one of the ship's crew. There was a fascinating surprise for us when we discovered that this ship had a Hurricane fighter plane and a catapult on board. The pilot was an R.A.F.-type sergeant and, in case of an aerial attack, he would take off and engage the enemy. If he survived combat, he either ditched the plane or found land.

We were beginning to appreciate the Merchant Service. Large convoys like ours had to be under constant alert; fifty Nazi submarines were in the area. Our four destroyers and eight corvettes were circling continuously around the one hundred merchant ships in our convoy. We dropped or catapulted many depth charges. By the fifth day, the excitement was growing and the crew were really scurrying about their duties, but there was no apparent panic. We were in the lead now of ten rows spread out as far as you could see. Suddenly, we saw our first casualty. An ammunition carrier blew up and we felt the blast, saw the flames and smoke and flying debris. We were told it was a direct hit with no survivors. Two more hits were recorded but we, as passengers, were getting no feed back. The corvettes were moving faster than ever and keeping up a constant hooting on their horn when suddenly, all went quiet. The enemy must have withdrawn. That was enough excitement for me for one day anyway, as I had done two shifts of torpedo watch from my post.

Our meals were served in style and the food was wonderful, especially after Air Force grub. We had table service and two Service Corps Sergeants who were supposed to teach us how to hold a knife and fork. I don't remember if I was amused or angry when these two "doughheads" would get too stoned. They had to be carried to their stateroom most nights. Whose idea was that anyway, Mackenzie King's?

Progress was slow and we were running into rough weather and heavy rain. The Captain ordered heavy ropes to be strung from stem to stern on each side of the ship as a safety precaution. The next day, the storm hit with a vengeance and the powers-that-be ordered the convoy abandoned. All ships were to be on their own, because they were too close together for safety in the convoy. The smaller ships could run with the storm, but the big ones like ours, with plenty of power, faced into the storm and rode it out. The power of the motors was one thing, but the strength of the waves was another. From wave to trough was at least fifty feet and, if we had not been facing into the wind, any one of those waves could have swamped us. It was most awesome and continued for almost three days. The dining room took a fair beating and the bartender had a little problem knowing which end to pour from. I, however, had no problem knowing which end to drink from. Tom Collins continued to champion the cause!

The plate glass on the deck in front of the wheel house was smashed — and that glass must have been one inch thick. The minute the storm moved in, we were ordered off the bridge. There would be no submarine attacks, which was a blessing, and poor visibility precluded air attacks. The ship picked up speed and we could feel the vibrations but, of course, there was no way for the passengers to know how far we were off track after the storm. Altogether, we spent sixteen days on board.

One day we spotted an aircraft, high above us, flying in our direction and the alert was sounded. The Captain came on the bridge and thanked us for being on our toes. When he arrived, I already had on my tin hat and was quite proud of myself. Although I thought the plane looked like a Sunderland, aircraft recognition was my worst subject, so I said nothing. The aircraft must have identified itself because the "all clear" sounded. The aircraft continued to circle for another hour and one of the crew said he was checking for subs and that we might be close to our destination. They didn't like subs following ships into harbour.

Finally the Sunderland, which it did indeed turn out to be,

tipped his wings and was gone. There was a crew of about ten on those planes. They were amphibian and could stay away for long periods on sub patrol and air/sea rescue work.

By now, nearly all the money was in the hands of the lucky. The poker games and crap games were slowing up, and I was desperately hanging on to a few quid for my Tom Collins, although I think I had my sea legs by now. There was no tax load here and they only cost a shilling. Why, that was cheaper than aspirin!

The twenty nurses who were supposed to be on board never did materialize, much to our disappointment.

Finally, it was announced that we would disembark in Belfast, Ireland the next day and that a pay officer would come on board for pay parade before leaving. Three rousing British cheers!

In those days, and at our age, most of us were quite unworldly about foreigners. There were quite a few Americans on board, separate from our group of Yanks, already recruited in Canada. There were also a dozen South American boys who had been recruited in their own countries to fight for Britain. They spoke no English, or very little, had playing cards with different pictures and symbols than ours, and colourful clothing that seemed strange to us. It was obvious these were outdoor types, not bank clerks.

We sighted land that evening, but did not approach, so we blacked out as usual and waited until early morning. The approach through the inlet to Belfast was one big hive of industry. This was a harbour loaded with ships of all types and sizes. Pay parade was held as promised, and our first pay in Sterling felt uncomfortable because we didn't yet understand the values.

When we left the docks, we went directly to the train station and waited. One of the men picked up a girl and carried on an animated conversation with her in a phone booth. When that conversation was over, there was nothing left to discuss. Time elapsed, three minutes. Good, no overtime! When she left the booth, everybody nearby clapped and cheered. I was getting a fast education watching all this.

We had a N.A.A.F.I. (Navy, Army, Air Force Inst.) bagged lunch at the station and waited for our train to take us to the ferry crossing for Stranraer. The fields along the way were a beautiful, lush green that we had never seen before. I think we must have travelled for forty miles with constant colour. When we arrived, the ferry was loading. It was huge and took all sorts of vehicles, plus hundreds of people. It had a very shallow draught and reminded me of a big dish pan of dirty dishes. A rough crossing would have been very uncomfortable indeed and there would have been plenty of sufferers. We sat on our dunnage bags and wondered, "What comes next?" It was a tiring journey with no Tom Collins. Luckily, though, I seemed to have gained my sea legs.

The activity along the Clyde was unbelievable, and it would seem that half of Britain's wartime supplies were coming in there. Everyone appeared cheerful and gave the Canucks a great welcome. Everything we had seen in the news reels was there. The working men and girls had a distinctive dress of their own — the men with their stubby peaked caps and the girls with the inevitable bandanna knotted on their hair. It made me feel we were fighting for the right team. As we travelled, we saw just how much damage the bombing had done and our admiration grew for these people.

We were advised that we were destined for the south coast of England and that we would be aboard the train overnight with light meals provided along the way. Orders were to sleep when we could, follow the blackout rules and don't talk to strangers. The walls have ears!

Before dark, we were able to see some of the rock-strewn landscape where the green growth was not very dense. Livestock were mostly sheep and cattle and it was not farm land as we knew it. As we moved south and crossed from Scotland into England, the farm land did slowly improve. We didn't really see the cities because of the blackout and even some of the signs were covered.

We were all slowing down a bit mentally and physically. We had been on the go a long time, but sleep didn't come easily; too much excitement, I guess. I had been fortunate and had a seat in a compartment along with five other men but, with our baggage in there too, it was pretty crowded. Eventually I did fall asleep and asked the usual question when I awoke, "Where are we?" I got the usual answer, "How the f—- would I know?" The following day, the train pulled into London and transferred us to another train bound for Bournemouth. The farmland in this part of England was much like that which we saw in Ireland — lush green pastures plus some lovely forest country. No rocky fields here.

As we neared the south coast, the population seemed to explode again. There were thousands of pretty homes and summer hotels basking in bright sunlight. The streets wound up and down hills and around curves and we were sure we must be close, at last, since our forward speed had dropped to about five miles per hour. Sure enough, a Bournemouth station sign appeared a minute or two later.

After disembarking, we marched alongside a van carrying baggage for about a mile to a building marked "The Bath Hotel." This turned out to be headquarters for Canadian Aircrews at Bournemouth at that time. Painted white and sitting on the slope of a rather steep hill, it had a commanding view of the sea and shore. Unfortunately the entire shoreline was mined and protected with barbed wire entanglements. Since "The Bath" did not have enough rooms for this contingent, a dozen of us were farmed out to sleep in other similar summer lodgings. We would get our meals at "The Bath" and report each morning at 9:00 a.m. for parade. The beauty of this was that we had single rooms with running water, lights and a gas meter for heat. The problem with the gas meter was it only ran for two hours and gobbled up a shilling each time unless you put a thread on your shilling and retrieved it. I was learning!

All the men in our course were transferred to the R.A.F. in preparation for four-engine bombers coming on stream within a year. They required an extra gunner per crew. In the meantime, we would require intensive turret and machine-gun training.

Bournemouth was a huge holding unit for British Empire Training Scheme graduates. All trained in Canada, these boys came from New Zealand, Australia, South Africa and Rhodesia, plus Canadians themselves with some Yanks who joined the R.C.A.F. in Canada. As well as making up a quarter of the R.A.F., Canadians also manned their own squadrons in England. The R.A.F. were leasing airfields and training their own recruits in

Canada as well. Altogether, we are talking about hundreds of thousands of men throughout the war. The Norwegians were also training their own pilots and had taken over Centre Island at Toronto, which became known as Little Norway.

The Second World War did more to bond Canada together than any other event to date. We had all been on the move back and forth across Canada learning about our neighbours. Here we were now in Bournemouth, England, readily accepting room mates from other countries and treating them as our own. The dozen that moved from "The Bath" to "The Wolsey" were made up of Australians, Rhodesians and Canadians. We tried to teach them Canadian, and they taught us Pitch Penny. According to one source, a boomerang was when you taught your wife to ride an ostrich and got her back again. Diverse? I'll say.

- CHAPTER 6 -

Bournemouth

While stationed at Bournemouth, we were issued with identification cards and ration cards. When we went to a restaurant or hotel, we presented the ration card and tokens were removed. Without these, we would not be fed. Most food was reasonable, but it was rationed. Cigarettes and sugar, or sugar products, were strictly rationed. In the restaurants, a popular sign read, "Stir well, we don't mind the noise."

Our routine never varied; we were paraded every morning and usually marched for an hour. These parades were conducted mostly by Army personnel and, by noon, they were through with us and we were on our own.

One day, I was wandering down the main street when I recognized Jack Alexander, my boyhood friend, on the other side. I called out to him and over he came. He said, "Have you got half a crown?" I gave it to him and he said, "Thanks!" and was gone. I hadn't seen him for a year and didn't see him again for four more. How's that for a short meaningful conversation with your best friend?

The greatest institution in Bournemouth was the Pavilion. This was a large dance floor and restaurant just back from the beach. It was circular in shape, with plenty of glass, and surrounded by magnificent shrubbery. You didn't have to take your girl there, you just met her there. Half the tables were taken over by pairs of young ladies. This was not a factory area, so most of them were well dressed office girls. Every Canadian in England knew about the Pavilion. It was heaven, pure heaven!

The next best place was the public bath house, originally built by the Romans. The building appeared to be about two hundred yards long with dozens of doors. You opened a door and put a penny in the slot then locked the outer door and got undressed. An unseen attendant would ask, "Warm or hot?" and out came the water, deep and hot. You tempered your bath with cold water and then you luxuriated.

One of our favourite drinking spots was the bar at the Metropole Hotel at Christchurch. Again, this was a landmark for Canadians and it was also a landmark for the Luftwaffe who were only twenty-five miles away and liked to sneak in low and drop a bomb or two. Then Lord Haw Haw would come on the radio for our noon laugh and tell us that he knew all about the Canadians in Bournemouth. The Germans figured, according to Haw Haw, that if they left us alone, we would drink ourselves to death. Good thinking!

Some of us finally got a week's leave and decided to see Loch Lomond, in Scotland. This entailed a long train ride with two transfers, one at London and another at Edinburgh. We then travelled on to Glasgow, which would soon become my home away from home. Loch Lomond was another twenty miles by bus. We arrived at the little village of Levin on the River Levin, but there was no tourist activity at all. Even the sightseeing bus was off, but we inquired and found that we could rent a flat-bottomed skiff and row up the river to Loch Lomond. Since my mother was from Scotland, I wrote and mailed a postcard from the general store, writing on it, "Just rowed up the River Levin." That's all!

We started to row up the river but, after about a hundred yards, we were waved over from one of the many boathouses on shore. They had spotted the Canadian flashes on our shoulders and brought out the stout, that very heavy malt beer. We felt that since it was a cool, dull day, the least we could do was to climb on board and participate. Two of these beers were almost impossible to drink in a hurry without poking them down with a broomstick, so we thanked the generous people and headed another hundred yards up the river. It was heavier going than we had anticipated and, when we passed the next boathouse, we accepted their hospitality quite readily and sat down to enjoy the reprieve. It didn't really matter that it was getting cool outside because we were feeling quite warm inside. The next stop was only fifty yards along, which was just as well since we were wandering off course a little. Our next hosts were equally as big hearted as the others but, by the time our noses were out of this foamy stuff, our resolve seemed to disappear and we decided we had gone far enough. With some help, we climbed in our skiff and let the wind do the work. It didn't take long before we hit close to the store with a thunk. We picked up what was left of our cash deposit and headed into the store to get warm while we waited for the bus.

I wrote another card which said, "Just rowed back again." Unfortunately, the second card arrived about two weeks ahead of the first one and I promptly heard from my father telling me to settle down!

I phoned my mother's sister, who lived just outside of Glasgow at Uddingston, and asked if she could put me up for a few days. She seemed pleased and told me what street tram to take. It was ten miles out, but no changes were required. With only one inquiry at the local grocery, I arrived safely.

What a wonderful person Aunt Jeannie was. She had three boys of her own, two from a previous marriage who were married and living on their own. The third and youngest, Ian, was first officer on a ship plying the India and Britain route. He held his Captain's papers and was studying for his Master's papers, which were evidently required to command a large ocean-going ship for a major shipping company. Ian was under thirty and still lived at home in Uddingston. Each trip he made to India he brought back a different sized carved ebony elephant with ivory tusks. Although I had never met him, this was a new world for me, and I was fascinated by the tales. His father, Uncle Johnny, was from the Orkneys and had been a sailor all his life. He was a sea Captain who had travelled all over the world. As a boy, he started on sailing ships and had enough fun in him to tell a story. Tall, strong featured and handsome would describe Captain John McCall.

They had bought their stone cottage when John retired some-where around 1937. When the Dunkirk disaster occurred, he volunteered to take a small ship to pick up survivors and brought them home safely. As the war intensified, his Company asked him if he would consider coming back to work and offered him the Dublin to Glasgow run. This was a very prestigious, but dangerous, crossing. He had accepted and had been active at this for the past two years. He was also in line for the top job of all as a pilot on the Clyde River.

Uddingston, to a Canadian, would have been considered a rock pile with a series of attractive old stone cottages on a stone road with stone fences and little gardens superimposed wherever possible. That was the outside appearance, but inside each cottage was the cosiest little house you can imagine. And yes, the teapot never left the stove top and the beds each had a down comforter.

When I asked Jeannie to take whatever ration coupons she needed, she told me she would take the book with her to the store and return it. Hardly any coupons were used. Johnny, it seems, could bring back all sorts of food from Dublin where there was no rationing because they were not at war. However, there were many thousands of Irish volunteers.

Two days later, I met my friends at the Locarno dance hall on Sachiehall Street, in Glasgow. This was a very famous place indeed. It had a large dancing area with hundreds of tables on three sides of the band shell. Balconies above suggested it might have been a playhouse at one time.

The most popular song of the year was, "I Don't Want To Set The World On Fire." Maybe not, but we kept adding fuel. That's when I first met "Scotty." Her real name was Isobel, but her nick-name stuck and our friendship grew over the years. She was trim and attractive and good company. She worked for a dry goods firm in town and, although I was never inside, she would tell me about her work as a buyer. She was three years older than I, but it made no difference at all. Scotty fitted in with my buddies that first day, which turned out to be an O.K. day — I now had her address and phone number.

The next day, Johnny had a day lay over so I stayed home

with him, or was it Jeannie's muffins? Anyway, I enjoyed this happy home, and it was such a change from a rather barren room in Bournemouth.

Jeannie told me I was to make this my home when I was in Scotland, and to bring a chum along. She sure understood boys, and she also knew our funds were limited.

The trains on the way back to Bournemouth were absolutely packed, especially the Flyer from Edinburgh to London. We could barely get through the aisles. But, once again, we were lucky and got a compartment. Some army girls got tired of standing outside our door and asked if we would trade for an hour. We very ungraciously said "No," but told them they could sit on our laps. That was one very busy compartment and the ticket master was also pretty busy sorting.

Christmas 1941 was coming up, but the festive season did not mean a great deal to me that year. I made sure I sent letters to Evelyn, Mom and Dad, and my friends back home. We were not yet on course so I did not have too much to tell. Some of the boys were beginning to move out, and I could guess our turn was not far away.

Our parades were still held every morning. One of the parade sergeants had laid a charge against me, but I am not certain what that charge was. I was paraded with one other man I did not know in front of about two thousand men and ticked off properly for five solid minutes. I don't know to this day what it was for and the R.S.M. was shouting so loudly I couldn't understand one word he said. It was a terrifying experience, and my ears still tingle. One thing for sure, I didn't argue!

My twenty-first birthday was coming up and I thought to myself that this past year had been busy enough for any young man. We knew Jimmy Jaycks, my room mate during the crossing, had just received a care parcel from home, because he had hidden it under his bed. We invited some W.A.F.'s to my birthday party and sicced them onto Jimmy, who was a proven sucker for this routine, and we all had a good time. We supplied the booze and Jimmy supplied the food — all ten pounds of it! All the girls had to do was invite him to the party because he certainly wouldn't have come just for us.

One of the dramatic moments in my life occurred when I wandered over to the mess hall for breakfast in the morning. The mess hall was located in The Bath Hotel and the walk over gave me time to breathe in a little fresh air following the night before. The shock came when I was offered half a cold kipper herring. This ugly beast still had its head on and the glassy eyes stared back at me. Try that on a belly full of beer!

There was a popular tea shop in Bournemouth where they served three-decker trays of little cakes and tarts and charged you for what was missing when you left. This was handy to where we were billeted and was an ideal place to meet people (translate that to mean girls). That's where I met Beryl Souch. Her home was in London, but she was working for the government on a temporary posting in an office in Bournemouth. Beryl had a girl friend, Betty, who was ten years her senior and acted more like a guardian than a friend. It was just as well, for Beryl was very young and very pretty. When we went to the Pavilion, Betty tagged along, but there was no way I could match her up with one of our boys. I came closer and closer to being in love with Beryl. When she folded into my arms on the dance floor, my head would spin.

Then, cold reality set in. I was posted to a place called Louth that I had never heard of before. It was near the Wash on the East Coast. Beryl had gone home to London for a few days and I had not been able to tell her personally. Maybe it was just as well, as all reports indicated that airgunners didn't last too long. This was a subject we never discussed except with other gunners. At twenty-one and healthy, I just couldn't picture myself as a casualty. Who me?

Quite a few boys from my original course at Mountainview (and on hold in Bournemouth) were also posted to Louth, including a bunch who trained out West. Total freedom was gone in Louth, except after supper when we were back in billets. Furthermore, this station was commanded by Army personnel and, just like Bournemouth, the C.O. was a very tough nut and a Colonel in the Guards. On top of all that, the course was very concentrated with aircraft recognition, armaments, gun sighting, air-to-air firing and air-to-ground firing. We had already been trained to fire from turrets, but a full five week turret course was to follow. We were

38

handling this quite well until our C.O. decided we needed drill and exercise. A notice was posted for us to appear the next morning at 8:00 a.m. on the drill square in shorts and running shoes. While this may sound reasonable, it was February and snow flakes where drifting down. This, plus our two unacknowledged petitions to the Mess Officer for better food (which was on the verge of rotting), made for a dangerous situation. The men just plain rebelled.

The C.O. left us standing on the parade ground for an hour. Usually this worked, but not this time. The C.O. then reminded us that, if we didn't follow orders, we were perpetrating a mutiny and could be court-martialled. That worked, but two of our men insisted that the Canadian Liaison Officer be called. The result was noticeable, and the two were not arrested for insubordination as I fully expected. The C.O. asked us to list our complaints and report the next morning. Parade was dismissed, cold knees and all.

The phone call to London to our staff headquarters prompted immediate action. They promised us a Liaison Officer would leave at once for Louth. This type of problem was a two edged sword and needed smoothing over right away. The war effort came first. Hurray for the war effort! The Canadian Liaison team of two arrived the following morning.

A list of our complaints was forwarded to the C.O., with copies to our Liaison Officers, and we then had to carry on with our schooling until called. At four o'clock, our Liaison Officers held a meeting with us behind closed doors and let us speak our minds. The fact that we were taking orders from men of equal or lesser rank bothered all of us more than anything else. We had been accustomed to taking orders from our own officers. The drilling business was petty, and we knew it, but there was no excuse for bad food. They reminded us that this was a local situation and we would soon be finished, so they suggested that we cool it since they had received promises of better conditions. If there were repercussions, they were to be advised immediately. We agreed to this and the problem faded away for the present.

If you get the feeling that our social life was suffering in Louth you would be right, although there were some high spots.

This was the first thatched roofed town I had ever been in and, when a local building required repairs, I sat down nearby and watched the thatching process. Before long, there were a dozen of our boys watching.

While we sat there, the local ladies brought us cups of tea and advised us they would be serving toast and fried mushrooms every afternoon, or later. Early evening was decided as best, because of our classes. Since it was too cool for growing mushrooms, I inquired and was told they had no problem preserving them and, surprise, surprise, one of the ladies, whose husband was in the "Middle East," was offering more than mushrooms! Her quaint way of letting one of us know was to say, "The kettle is boiling."

There must have been a dozen pubs in Louth. The local men were a quiet lot, but the publicans would chatter away. This was a rural area with no industry. There might have been a movie house, but I never saw it. There might also have been a main street, but I never saw that either.

- CHAPTER 7 -

Bournemouth & Louth
March 1942

The day before the course ended, we were advised that we would be going on indefinite leave, so to be sure and leave a forwarding address. This was a most unusual announcement and the reasons given were that the courses ahead of us had backed up and the new four-engine bombers that required our services were a month behind. We didn't mind a month off, but how would we finance ourselves away from the base? We were all in the same boat — insufficient funds. We decided to hold a giant crap game so at least those who won could afford to go on leave. To make a short story long, two of us won all the money. The other one was Jack Cameron. I had a phone call from Cam the other day. "Do you know," he said, "that it is fifty years ago since I met you ... and furthermore, those have been the worst fifty years of my life!" Then he hung up.

Cam and I decided to go on leave together, but first we headed down to the Post Office Savings Office to open our respective accounts by dumping all those beautiful pound notes on the counter. This made the clerk laugh, and it made us laugh, and for the next thirty days we laughed. The beauty of the Post Office Savings was that you could withdraw your money in any town in the British Isles — but only two pounds per day, each. This was perfect and we would never run out.

Cam was a Toronto boy from the West End. That was my

41

second mistake. Then, he asked me if I drank beer, and that was my third mistake.

I had only one forwarding address and Jack had none, so we headed up to Jeannie's by a circuitous route. First we went to Bournemouth where I could sic Cam on to Beryl's girl friend. Cam never got too carried away because he had a girl back home, and this worked out just fine. We spent a few days together with the girls but, during the daytime, they both had to work. I told Beryl I couldn't give her a new address yet, but I would let her know. She had trouble believing this.

Cam and I headed for London and then took the train north to Edinburgh on our way to Glasgow. More and more Polish Flyers were showing up in Scotland, and it was interesting to see the cross-section of these men on the trains. They were certainly dynamic, and had only one mission — to shoot down Germans! It turned out most of their squadron were operating from Scottish bases. There had been many Polish/Scottish weddings already, since the Poles had been in Scotland since 1940.

The kids today use a lot of perfume (call it cologne or lotion, if you like), but nothing compared to the Poles. A common comparison in popular use at the time was "smelling like a whore at a wedding." Each Polish Flyer claimed to be of noble birth, and tried to act accordingly. We suggested they post signs at the Locarno which would read, "All Polish officers are to check their swords before going on the dance floor."

It was that time of year when the greenery was at its best and, in this rolling countryside, we had a new picture every few minutes. As we came to the Scottish border area, it began to change to a gorse-like growth and was not so colourful until the fresh weather came on, but still, it was an interesting panorama with sheep dotting the landscape.

I had written to Jeannie to warn her of our plans before leaving Louth. When I phoned her after we got off the train, she was pleased that we were coming and welcomed Cam to stay as long as he wished. Jeannie seemed happy to see us and immediately made Cam feel at home. I told her I was her nephew, not Cam, and not to spoil him, but I think she did anyway. Can't win them all! It was evening hours when we arrived and Johnny was home.

What a wonderful, warm feeling. Top up that tea pot, two of your boys are home!

With thirty clear days ahead, we figured we could see some of the area and, next morning, wandered around downtown. After a couple of hours, we decided it was impossible to support all of these merchants and we should narrow it down to the local pub. Everywhere we found our Canadian badges brought a smile of friendship or a twinkle in the eye and began to wonder what the gang ahead of us had been up to. Glasgow was the first time I was approached with a very famous line, "Hey, Mac, wanna buy a gold watch? How about a diamond ring?" All the time this shady hustler was opening his jacket or pushing up a sleeve. This sleeve really intrigued me since there must have been a dozen watches on one arm. Having no luck with me, he sort of disappeared into an alleyway.

We were gone from Uddingston each day from mid morning until late evening. We got to know the girls on the last trolley which left Glasgow for Uddingston at ten o'clock and had some good laughs with them. Often we were the last riders, since it was wartime and everybody worked long hours and turned in early. Then it happened, as it was bound to, that we missed the last trolley. We were sitting forlornly on the curb when a trolley marked "barns" went by with one of our acquaintances aboard. They stopped and, after holding a conference, the driver said to hop on and then spent five minutes with our conductor, Maggie, discussing how to get to Uddingston without getting stopped. They must have decided that speed was the answer because we took off at one hell of a clip. Why, it was enough to sober both of us. Jack hung on to Maggie since he got there first and the driver was laughing and singing and making announcements such as, "Only eight miles to go." It wasn't the forward motion that rattled me, it was the swaying. On one curve I figured we would leave the tracks and head right through the front gates of a local marble orchard. But, no, we hung on. Cam, I noticed, was doing some fair hanging on too.

We arrived in Uddingston before 11:00 p.m., even counting curb sitting time. We tried to tip our friends, but they wouldn't have any part of it. We have since wondered what trouble they really got into since the trip was all on their own time.

Our well balanced suppers called for fish and chips most nights and these were real fish and chips, none of this paper thin stuff. The deluxe package was available in a choice of newspaper wrappers — today's or yesterday's. All this for pennies! We seldom got back to Jeannie's for supper and we ate our fish and chips in the park. Individual meat pies were also available on Sachiehall Street, further down. We didn't worry about fluids, there would be plenty to follow. We were never late for the Locarno though!

By our third day in Scotland, I hadn't yet phoned Scotty. I had assumed that she had another boyfriend, but I was pleased when she agreed to see us at the Locarno. Cam had never met her.

About a quarter of the dancers came in formal attire. I was told that, prior to the war, everybody dressed for public dancing. One thing about a uniform, it covered that situation completely. Waltzes were still popular and, on this huge dance floor, there was plenty of scope for twirling. The tango was next in popularity and "I Don't Want to Set the World on Fire" was a runaway to the top of the charts. Nearly all the music was from North America, with the exception of wartime favourites, like "White Cliffs of Dover."

With so many young men away in the forces, the young ladies had little choice but to stay home or get a girlfriend and head to the dances. Almost all of the girls went stag. The Locarno was so large that it seemed as if half of the city went there in the evenings.

Isobel Thomson arrived as planned and it was good to see her. She was about five feet, three inches, with a terrific slim figure. I hadn't seen her for at least three months and I still called her Scotty, which she didn't seem to mind. Cam liked her and told me so. I think this meant he preferred her to Beryl in London, but I didn't ask.

Evening entertainment opportunities were very limited — a show, a dance or a pub. There was a skating rink at nearby Paisley where you could rent ice skates; Cam and I tried it. This made for a pleasant afternoon despite the fact that there was not a very good edge on the skates. Before the war, they played league hockey here and one of the teams was made up of expatriated

Canucks. They were very popular competitors. The people here found it difficult to believe that most Canadians could skate and most of the boys played hockey.

Time for a spot of supper? How does a pickled onion, a bit of white bread and a pickled egg sound? It was then just about time to meet Scotty at the Locarno. We felt we might have a few more days leave left, and I thought we should complete our Edinburgh plans. An early morning trip would have been better, but we never did build up any cash, and had to wait for the Post Office Bank to open. The clerks had obviously been watching our assets dwindle. They got the biggest charge out of our withdrawals and our nonchalant attitude towards pending financial disaster.

We were aboard the train for Edinburgh by noon and travelling light. This meant a toothbrush, comb, razor and soap. Once again, the Polish Flyers were on the move. There must have been a dozen on our coach alone and Woolworth must have had a fresh shipment of Lilac Cologne and been sold out by train time.

While visiting a childhood friend of my mother's in Edinburgh, I received a telegram telling me to report to Stormy Downs in Wales on a date which had already passed. This made me absent without leave and I could have been charged. Fortunately, the arrival date of the telegram was marked so I phoned Stormy Downs to straighten this mess out. It wasn't easy. They didn't want to believe me; a malingering Canuck was right up their alley so I told them I would bring proof with me. I asked for a travel warrant and was told it would be waiting at the station. I said I would leave early the next morning and was told to "Leave now." I replied that I couldn't leave without a train and that shut them up. In the meantime, they planned to check my records, which were not entirely spotless, and I didn't know if there was a night train or not.

Cam, meanwhile, had not yet received his telegram and could stay until he did. This meant he was going to a different station, unfortunately, so I had to say goodbye to everybody and head out early.

- CHAPTER 8 -

Stormy Downs

Back home, my former girlfriends were gradually getting married off. Ralph Johnson, Johnny Slatter, and Doug Appleton were heading overseas. Slatter's recent letter, which had just caught up to me, indicated he would be in the Middle East. I had completely lost track of so many of my class mates who had joined up.

A letter from my father told me that Evelyn was having a tough struggle and was losing a great deal of weight. This in turn was very hard on Mom. I felt so helpless! No name had ever been mentioned as to what the illness could be. I suspected more and more that it was tuberculosis, for which there was not yet a sure cure available to the public.

My trip to Stormy Downs was long and torturous with three transfers. There was interesting new country to see here with lots of lakes and green, moss-like, rock cover. While sitting on the train, I fell to dreaming for awhile about my own future and how much more knowledge I needed, since I would soon be flying against enemy targets and fighter planes. Reports from other gunners who were travelling added twinges of fear, but they didn't last, fortunately. Besides, none of the ones on operations that I met seemed to have much experience. Little did I know that they didn't last long enough to get much experience. None of our training officers had ever mentioned this fact.

Welsh names were beginning to appear before me at the

stations now, so I probably didn't have that much further to go. Pronunciation was impossible for me, but my destination read Llanelly and eventually it showed up. A van from Stormy Downs was there to meet the train and picked up quite a number of Air Force members.

Sure enough, the M.P.'s were hot to trot when they checked me in and tried to put me over the coals. The time of arrival on the telegram covered me. I told them I would need a meal and a billet. My dunnage bag was still with me also. They found my squad and turned me over to the N.C.O in charge.

Right away, I found some of my old mates and relaxed. Stowing my kit, I headed to the mess hall to eat with a new chum tagging along. He told me that it was an O.K. station with a minimum of B.S. The course had actually started two days ago, but nothing heavy yet. Turret flying would begin after we learned more about the mechanics involved. This constituted the total armament at the time on four-engine bombing aircraft planes in the R.A.F.

At Stormy Downs, we had Bolton Paul Turrets, where the controls and gun fire worked like a joystick, and Fraser Nash Turrets, that worked from short bicycle type handles and were in general use in all the new four-engine aircraft, the Wellingtons, and maybe other aircraft as well.

Our training staff here were operational people who knew the score and drilled as much into us as they could, because they were aware that our lives depended on it. As an example, in the armourers section we learned to take a Browning Machine gun apart with our eyes shut and attempt to put it back together again in the same way. If a gun jammed at night, we could now correct it. We learned how to pattern the aim of our guns and the best distance for the fire power from the four guns to converge. Since much of our work would be in the dark, we had to memorize where our repair tools would be placed beside us and, above all, how to release the turret doors in an emergency. Then we practised the loading sequence for our guns. Our long tracks of bullets had to be reviewed for free running action. We also learned "bail out procedure" and "dingy inflation and releasing procedures." That took up our mornings. Our afternoons were now open for flying.

We hadn't forgotten our social commitments to the local girls altogether. The Welsh girls must have been warned about the Air Force guys though. A young lady in Llanelly told me she would have to ask her mother's permission to go for a walk with a Canadian. When I arrived, Mother stood one foot above me and said in a very loud voice, "What are your intentions?" Do you know, I found this very hard to answer.

Most of our evenings were spent in the N.C.O. mess or in Llanelly at the local pub. We were pretty darn tired when our day was over. We were getting a lot of flying time now, and our target scores were improving. The most exciting part followed when three Spitfires from another drome were sent up to "attack" us. Our armourers had done a safety check on our guns before take-off, just to be sure we didn't get a direct hit on our own planes by mistake. The odds on this would be long, believe me! This flying was done over the Spit and Cornwall which, by air, was not very far from our station.

We flew for three more days, mostly air-to-ground. I had done this work at two stations before this, but never from a turret. It was a new skill to be learned.

We were advised in advance that no leaves would be granted at the end of this course, only a forty-eight hour pass. Our move was only a few days away, but there was no telling where. This move would be our last station before going to a squadron.

- CHAPTER 9 -

Upper Heyford, Oxfordshire

Our move took us to #16 Operational Training Unit at Upper Heyford. This was a permanent force unit and would be our home for about two months. There were not sufficient rooms for us on the station, so billets were supplied at the local manor house. The owners had moved to smaller quarters for the duration of the war.

This was the beginning of May, 1942. May, in my mind, is Britain's best month. The green growth is lush and the flowers are everywhere. It is impossible for me to describe the beauty of the village of Upper Heyford, near Oxford. All the buildings, except the manor house, were thatched. We each signed out a bicycle from stores to get us back and forth to the airdrome, which was five miles away. As at Louth, the local ladies prepared mushrooms on toast for a penny but, better still, a bunch of Womens' Army Air Force (W.A.A.F.) had heard there was a new course moving in. They came out to say hello. We had thought we were going to be isolated, but not anymore.

That evening I met a wonderful girl named Kay, who became my constant companion in all my leisure hours. She was attractive, but not beautiful. We would ride through the countryside each evening and I do believe she was as happy as I was, and needed the companionship as much as I did, even though we both knew this would be a short friendship. I never asked her, but I had a feeling she had lost a fiancee or a husband in the Air Force and this made our friendship more important. She never asked me questions either.

On our first day at the station, we went on pay parade (hurrah), dental parade (boo) and equipment stores parade (reserved judgement). We were issued a locker and key in the flying room, thin silk gloves, a fleece lined flying jacket and new flying boots in preparation for flying training. A coverall flying suit was then added. Parachutes were drawn daily and returned for replacement after all flights.

The next day was the most important of my life. We were invited to attend an Aircrew meeting to include all the trades. We were to find our own crew members among these men. I poured a coffee and began looking around without committing myself. There was one Canadian pilot who appealed to me and I said "Hello." His name was McNichol, and he seemed pretty steady. After a minute, I wandered off and spoke to other pilots. A navigator/observer and a wireless operator approached me and we talked for a minute. Finally, one of them said, "Would you like to meet our new pilot?" and I agreed. It turned out to be McNichol, who had directed them to me. I agreed to team up. For the next year, my life would depend on McNichol's abilities and I never regretted my decision. From then on, we operated as a team. At Upper Heyford, we flew in Hampdens for gunnery, but mostly on Wellingtons for cross-country. The Wellington I.C. was a wonderful aircraft, but very slow and underpowered.

There were five of us now. Glen McNichol, our pilot, had been brought up on his father's wheat farm, out West, and was used to wrestling with big machines. That made him the perfect match-up for a heavy bomber. His home was Richlea, Saskatchewan. George Bishop, our bomb aimer, was from just south of Owen Sound, Ontario. He was a fully qualified observer which combined bomb aiming with navigation. McNichol, Bishop and I were all old men of twenty-one. Harold Henry Francois Jean de Beaupre — "Bo" — was our navigator from Waterloo, Ontario. He also was a fully qualified observer, which might call for a separation of Bishop and Beaupre if ordered. MacFarlane, our wireless operator, was the only married member of our crew and had proved himself already. His wife was expecting any minute. She was very attractive and this is the real reason why we kept MacFarlane.

There was the nucleus of a very long lasting and productive crew with whom I was pleased to serve, although I would never have admitted it at the time. We were not accustomed to complimenting each other — just the opposite.

Each day at 11:00 a.m., we took off for practice flying as a crew. Nic, as McNichol was called, already had several hours flying in Wellingtons and handled them very well. They were most reliable. We tried everything to get the feel of the aircraft, including low flying which was frowned upon. We were back by noon, had some lunch and checked the board for individual instructions. The navigators were the busiest. About every second day, a class would be held on gunnery and aircraft recognition. Canadian gunners had practically no instruction on aircraft recognition back home. We knew the names of the German aircraft, but not the wing span or the other statistics that were so vital when firing our guns with gyro sights.

We had supper in town one evening and let our hair down a bit. This was a learning process. We were all new to each other, but I felt at ease with each one of them. After lunch in the N.C.O. mess, we played a hand of bridge. Nic and I took on McFarlane and Bo. This became an on-going affair. Bo was the most experienced and, although I had played whist all my life, I had to learn bridge in a hurry. I have played ever since.

There were three mess halls where all our meals were served: the Officers' Mess, which also contained a lounge and bar and was for officers and their guests only; the Non-Commissioned Officers' Mess was for senior N.C.O's only (Sergeant, Flight Sergeant and Warrant Officers); and the Enlisted Mess Dining Hall. There was absolutely no cross-over allowed between messes. The N.C.O. Mess was large and very comfortable. There were dozens of leather covered arm chairs and many chesterfields. At this time in the war, most Aircrew recruits arriving at an Operational Training Unit were N.C.O's. A year from now, most recruits would be officers.

When I rode my bicycle back to Upper Heyford for the

evening, I hoped that Kay would show up. I noticed a fair number of W.A.A.F.'s were there already and my spirits sank. A half hour later, two hands covered my eyes from behind and I didn't have to ask who it was. My happiness must have shown for there was Kay looking wonderful and asking where my bike was so we could head out. I guess we were all lonely, dreadfully lonely.

We rode along quietly for a while and she was a little ahead of me with her shirt tails out and flapping in the breeze. There seemed to be little of interest on this road except for something on the left in the distance and, of course, Kay herself, who was very interesting indeed. When we were opposite a haystack, Kay called over, "Maybe we should rest awhile..."

There was some nasty news on the radio the next day. The Germans had made a mass bombing attack on Coventry, which was not that far away by Canadian standards. This beautiful city, noted for its cathedral, was just about obliterated and there were thousands of casualties. Coventry was not a prime military target and this was a cold blooded massacre. Anything the R.A.F. did from now until the end of hostilities would pale beside this sickening affair. It was also the biggest mistake Hitler ever made. The British people gathered around the flag, possibly as never before, and the bombing prompted Churchill's famous speech, "We will send one thousand bombers ... " And we did.

The problem at the moment was that we didn't have one thousand operational aircraft in all of Britain, or crews either. Operational Training Units had to supply crews and aircraft to make up the shortage. In our own case, one concession was made. Our pilot would be temporarily replaced by Squadron Leader Couch, who had thousands of hours flying Wimpeys (the affectionate nickname for Wellingtons), but no experience on operations at all.

We worked quickly to get fully equipped. S/L Couch himself accompanied me to stores to be sure I had the necessary protective clothing for operational flying. My location in the rear turret exposed me to outside air, sometimes as low as sixty degrees below zero. The centre turret panel was removed for better vision. I picked up an electrically wired jacket with gloves and slippers attached. This was worn over the uniform jacket, but under the

52

flying suit. Silk gloves were worn next to the skin because, if bare hands touched the metal parts of the turret, they would stick and freeze. Parachutes would be picked up just prior to take-off and we already had our helmets in our lockers.

Each morning at 11:00 a.m., the lorry picked us up and drove us to the aircraft. We taxied past the firing butts where the gunner could check his guns, and then took off for a thirty minute instrument check. If we were to fly that night, a briefing time would be posted for us all together.

The excitement was growing, but there was still no word yet. In the afternoon, we were confined to base and warned not to phone out. Then it came — briefing at 6:00 p.m. Some of the instructors at Upper Heyford had finished a tour, but most of us would be on our first operation against the enemy.

Briefing, in itself, was an education. There were guards posted all around the briefing room and wall charts were covered. There were several officers sitting on the platform waiting for all the crews to arrive and for the Commanding Officer to appear. Finally the waves parted and in came the C.O. Everyone stood. Most crew members sat near their own crew and we wondered, of course, where we would be sent.

"Gentlemen, the target for tonight will be Cologne." Cologne was in the Rhine Valley, the most heavily defended area in Germany with hundreds of fighters available and F.L.A.K. batteries surrounding the entire city. The aircraft from Upper Heyford would leave base early because they were twin-engine only and could not keep up with the speed of four-engine Lancasters, Sterlings and Halifaxes, which would make up the bulk of the raid. Another problem would be the fact that our maximum height, fully loaded, would be eleven thousand feet. The weather officer reported heavy cloud, but an opening was expected over the target one hour ahead of arrival. This cover would protect the aircraft at twenty thousand feet, but, unfortunately, not those at ten thousand.

We were flying I.C. Wellingtons, a very early variety, but with an excellent rating for reliability. A word of caution came from the briefing officer that we would probably lose more planes on take-off, due to a lack of power, than we would over the target area.

Lancaster cockpit

This would be due to a heavy bomb load. The picnic was obviously over!

After briefing, our crew headed to the mess hall for supper and then moved over to the lounge to play a quiet game of bridge. McFarlane, or "Mac," headed out to the flying room stores and drew our chocolate bar ration, something which the rest of us seemed to know nothing about. It was nearly impossible to get a chocolate bar off station, and we got two bars per man for operational sustenance. Our bridge game was rather ragged that evening and the whole mess hall became pretty quiet. The van would be along at 9:30 p.m. Being new, most of us did not know what to expect.

The lorries began to arrive and, one by one, the crews headed out. Once in the lorry, Bo told me there was new navigational equipment aboard. Very hush, hush! There was a DESTRUCT button on all new navigational aids so that, if we had to abandon the aircraft, it would not fall into enemy hands. Both Mac and Bo now had buttons.

The first stop was parachute stores and then out to the aircraft. They were taking no chances. We were there an hour-and-a-half early. This was apparently so we would have enough time to get nervous.

It was now May 30, 1942. It had taken us a year-and-a-half to progress this far.

As a crew, we reviewed our escape hatch procedure, our parachute procedure and our dinghy procedure. On my own, I checked the turret doors and hundreds of feet of 303 bullet tracks. Then I checked the gun sight, which was "tuned in" to both of my turrets' Browning machine guns and, finally, I made sure the cocking togo was handy.

It was full moonlight here, and about thirty minutes to start up. We were wearing quite a bit of clothing and did not want to get overheated, so we went out and sat on the grass nearby. Everybody lit up a cigarette. We were all a bit pensive, I think, and we just tried to relax.

Squadron Leader Couch suggested we get on board now. We were not used to orders given in such a polite manner but we went anyway — I thought I could like this man. Our pilot called for chocks and revved his motors one at a time. There was a great deal of noise as each of the eleven other aircraft in our make-up squadron did the same. Each crew member, in turn, called the pilot to confirm his intercom connection was working and was acknowledged. The chocks were pulled away and our aircraft joined the line-up for take-off. (You're lucky I wasn't a pilot or this list would have taken ten more paragraphs. I'm ready for take-off, I don't know about you.)

We were rolling now and I turned my turret on the beam so I wouldn't be trapped if we crashed. The speed picked up, my turret began to bounce a bit, and then we were off the ground and slowly gaining height. It seemed that Squadron Leader Couch could fly a Wimpey!

To bring the aircraft up to operational height was a long, slow process, and it took nearly our total trip across the water to do this. Finally, land was up ahead and was clearly visible. The odd line of tracer curved across the sky, and there were some flak bursts. We had our height now and were flying along between ten thousand and eleven thousand feet, heading straight into Germany. It would still be another hour before we were at the target.

Our oxygen was on now and S/L Couch decided it was time for evasive action. He must have read about this in a comic book judging by his antics. It was just as well I had tested my guns over the North Sea or I might have caught up with my own bullets! I believe all he did was attract attention from the searchlight batteries below. I hadn't spotted a fighter yet, but one particular searchlight seemed to be flicking closer until he finally pinned on and up came the flak. The bursts sounded like someone eating apples in church. Quickly, they swung the master light on to us and then we were being blinded by ten searchlights. By now, they knew our speed, direction and height, and would set up a box. Our pilot very cooly told us to hang on. He was going to dive right down the master light beam. Then he temporarily lost control and went into a spin, over corrected and spun the other way. Finally, we pulled out at four thousand feet, having shaken off the searchlights.

I was a mess, my vision was completely gone and I called

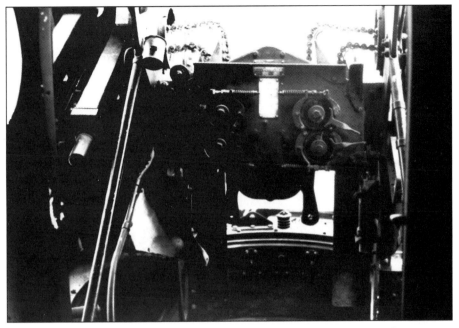

Rear turret of Lancaster.

View from turret of Lancaster

through on the intercom to advise the pilot. How he had been able to pull out with a full bomb load, I will never know, but while they were having their jolly little spin up front, I was being whiplashed out back. It took a long time to climb back to bombing height, but I didn't care. Over the target I didn't care, and when our bombs went down, I didn't care. It took two hours for my vision to come back and some semblance of sensibility to return.

On our return, we were sent directly for debriefing. Ten of our aircraft were back, and there were a lot of officers in the room trying to take statements from each crew member. This was a big night on a training unit, where only half of the men had ever been on OPS. We had a tot of blackstrap rum coming to us and then our bacon and eggs. Blackstrap rum usually did wonders for me, regardless of what others thought of it, but I had never used it to correct vision before. Wonderful stuff! Breakfast at four o'clock in the morning was merely a question of getting it down before I fell asleep and eggs were so scarce they were only served to Aircrews.

I was the only member of our crew staying at the manor house in the village, so I phoned Nic and found we were not on duty until the following day at 11:00 a.m. for our usual flight check. He also advised me that the Cologne raid had been a success — a success with forty-one aircraft missing. I went back to my cot until about 3:00 p.m., then rode my bike to the mess where I stayed until supper time. There was a stud poker game in progress, which was easy to break into since everybody wanted your money. We chipped in for a two gallon pail of lager and settled in for a couple of hours. When supper time arrived, I hadn't accumulated enough to retire on, but at least I wasn't down, and I could afford the two pence for mushrooms on toast at the manor when Kay got off duty.

It was a five mile ride back to the manor and it gave me time to reflect a little. In this lovely rural setting I found I was able to divorce the war from my private life and relax, if only for a little while, waiting for Kay to arrive.

The ladies came around the large circle that had formed and served our snack of toast and mushrooms. Then there was an impromptu sing-song before the W.A.A.F.'s teamed up with our gang and went walking. Within five minutes you could have been lonely!

Kay and I decided to use our bikes. When we arrived at the cross-roads at the edge of the village, I complained to Kay that there was a problem with my steering; it always wanted to turn left ... which, of course, was the road to the haystack.

By eleven the next morning, we were back in the air doing "locals," our regular aircraft checks on instruments, gauges and the working and moving parts of the aircraft while flying. These had already been thoroughly checked on the ground by the maintenance crews. The guns had been stripped and cleaned. The turrets were hydraulic with the power supplied by one of the motors. The pressure in these lines was adjusted by the armourers, and this was of vital importance or the guns would not aim and the turret would not move. Enemy gun fire often punctured the oil lines and made turrets useless.

When we landed, we were once again told to "stand by," because we would be flying. Briefing was held at 3:00 p.m. and the target was revealed as Essen, another of the Rhur cities which was even more heavily defended than Cologne. This would be the second of the one thousand bomber raids promised by Winston Churchill. It was now June 1, 1942, and just forty-eight hours after the Cologne raid.

The bulletin board back at the mess listed the names of the boys missing after the Cologne raid. Two of the gunners were from our own course, but we had not had time to get to know the men they flew with. The forty-one aircraft lost at Cologne represented a total of about two hundred and fifty men lost.

Essen was well protected by cloud cover. Thousands of searchlights were in play and, when an aircraft nearby us was coned, we slipped through beside it. The cloud cover above us was at about sixteen thousand feet and, although most of our bombers were flying above that, neither the older Wellingtons nor the Whitleys could reach that height. Fighters were not a problem for the moment because the flak was so intense they might have been hit by their own shells. The German fighters also hesitated to attack an aircraft on the way in to the target, since the explosion from a direct hit would also destroy them due to the bomb load on board. Although we would be easier `pickin's' for the fighters later on, we were able to see our target and unload our bombs quickly. Our speed increased considerably once the bombs were gone. George Bishop, or `Bish' as we knew him, directed the pilot from his bomb sight position while lying on the floor with a small window below him. We waited tensely for the `bombs gone' signal, and then breathed easier.

An ME110 picked us up on our way home, but we spotted him first. I gave him a burst of about fifty rounds, which seemed to discourage him from attacking. From then on, our return trip was uneventful. Hurry along fellahs, I thought, my tot of rum awaits me!

Whereas Cologne was a big success, Essen was not. There had been too much cloud interference for good bombing results, so the bombs were too scattered.

The following facts may give you a better idea of the aircraft involved in those first two of the thousand bomber raids that Churchill had promised Hitler. Some of them were modern and up-to-date while others, by now, were "oldies," but necessary to live up to our pronouncement.

COLOGNE	ESSEN
28 Whitleys	29 Whitleys
79 Hampdens	71 Hampdens
46 Manchesters	33 Manchesters
602 Wellingtons	545 Wellingtons
88 Stirlings	77 Stirlings
131 Halifaxes	127 Halifaxes
73 Lancasters	74 Lancasters
1047 Aircraft	956 Aircraft
41 Aircraft lost	31 Aircraft lost

The moon period, when bombing conditions were ideal, had come to an end and it would be a few weeks until ideal conditions prevailed again. Consequently, as a crew, we had a week's rotation leave coming to us and decided to go to Glasgow. The other crew members all had their own connections there, but I preferred to stay at Jeannie's. Mac, of course, lived there with his family. I noted the address and promised to meet them at the Locarno. I phoned Jeannie to confirm my stay before I headed out with the others. I had packed a very light bag at the manor house and left a message for Kay that all was okay. I had saved two chocolate bars for Scotty and hoped they wouldn't melt. Silk stockings and chocolate bars both had a great deal of appeal in Britain. One of our American boys had requested his whole overseas parcel be made up of silk stockings! And that reminds me of the young man on his honeymoon who ordered a gross of `them thar things' from a druggist on a Friday. By Monday, he was back complaining there was only 143 in the box. The druggist went and got him one more and said, "Sorry, I hope I didn't spoil your weekend." Whoops, sorry Mom!

There were the Canadians — Bo, Bish, Nic and I — plus Mac in one compartment. It didn't take a whole compartment to hold us. There had been a girl on the platform with four sailors crowded around her and Nic made room for her, but not the four sailors. Good company all the way to Edinburgh! So far we hadn't even mentioned our first two OPS or the crews we lost those nights. It was better that way for awhile, until we learned to handle it night after night.

It was good to be back in Glasgow for a few days, and a treat to be at Aunt Jeannie's cottage in Uddingston. The middle of June was warm and pleasant and just strolling about felt good. I gave my ration book to Jeannie to use. We spent the day drinking tea and talking. There never seemed anything she wanted me to do for her around the house. I phoned Scotty at her office and arranged to meet her that evening at the Locarno. She was always good company and accepted the way I flitted in and out of her life without much advance notice. More than once, I told myself, I could do worse.

MacFarlane stayed home with his new family, but Bo and Nic were at the Locarno which, in turn, meant I didn't get many dances with Scotty. To fly and live with these guys was one thing, to go dancing was another. They kept Scotty pretty well monopolized, but I did shine later after they were gone, I must admit.

The following day there was an invitation to Mac's home for supper. His wife was very lovely and, of course, they now had a new arrival. I would have liked to ask her how she accepted the risk involved in Mac's work, but then I reconsidered. If she was not aware just what the odds were, I was darn sure I wasn't going to be the one to tell her. It did help me to decide for myself, though, that I would make no long range commitments while on operations. Mac was a good host and we enjoyed the meal. After supper, some of Mac's friends dropped in and we had a house party on our hands. It had been a long time.

Back at Upper Heyford, we were put on an intensive low level flying routine every day for ten days. I also had gunnery practice, air-to-air and air-to-sea in both Wellingtons and Hampdens. Hampdens seemed very manoeuvrable, but I liked the stability of the Wellingtons better.

The moon period was building up again and, although we were still in training, a third, one thousand bomber raid was rumoured. If so, we would know within a day or two.

Back at the Manor House, they had a visit from the Billeting Officer in my absence. Unfortunately, there were a few W.A.A.F.'s in the building and charges were about to be laid. The boys put up a great fight and explained that they were stranded there and hadn't complained, but they must be allowed some visitors! It turned out they had a very understanding young officer who finally agreed to ignore the situation. His parting shot, however, was addressed to one of the girls, "Do up that brassiere!" The Manor House belonged to nobility and was on wartime loan. The description I received was that the girl belonged because she was so nobly built.

I was already on my second piece of toast and mushrooms when Kay arrived. I had not been able to see much of her due to our training schedule but, in her own quiet way, she had a knack for making me happy. Even her smile could do it. She knew that my course was nearly over and that I wouldn't be there much longer. She accepted that fact, and it was a wonderful evening!

Next morning we were back on alert. We did our locals at 11:00 a.m. and were back at noon, just as the station went on full security. At 3:00 p.m., we were briefed for Bremen, which was a big, important target. Bremen was heavily industrialized and a major sea port. Our round trip would be at least two hundred miles farther than to either Cologne or Essen. The briefing officer did his best to try to scare us to death with his story of how heavily defended Bremen was but, seeing we had to go regardless, we just tried to pick the weak spots for ourselves. Again, I had another pilot with Nic as second dickie. I was sure glad Nic was there, though, because I had the utmost confidence in him. The first pilot, Flight Sergeant McGinlay, I did not even know.

In our super speedy Wellington I.C.'s, it was about a seven hour trip, so we had to take off early. The Lancasters could do the same trip in five hours. One thing about our I.C. though, we could see the target better. We should, we were two miles closer to it! Our operational height was ten thousand feet, as usual. The Lancasters were at twenty to twenty-two thousand feet.

The searchlights were certainly thick and seemed to ring most of the city of Bremen. Cloud cover above was far too thick for the heavy bombers to stay at their usual height. We would have been in as much danger from bombs from above, hitting our aircraft, as from the flak guns below. One good thing the search-lights did was cast a glimmer of light on the river surface and give us a bearing. Bo had brought us to the Weser River, bang on. Bish advised the pilot to change from evasive action to steady. He had found the target straight ahead. We then started our bomb run, which made for a scary last ten seconds, then, 'bombs away." We turned sharply to head out of the target area and resumed our weaving pattern of flight so that a fighter could not pick us off with his 20M cannon shells without some effort. Most German fighters using cannons were set up to zero in at one thousand yards. Our 303 Brownings were set up for three hundred yards for the simple reason that, in the dark of the night, we couldn't see beyond three hundred yards, but early morning light increased this and put us at a disadvantage.

The next hour was the most dangerous, as the fighters sat back waiting in the clouds above. An aircraft nearby suddenly exploded and I could see the fighter pulling away. I watched for parachutes, but only saw one. Keep flying McGinlay! There was nothing we could do.

We were back at the drome by 3:00 a.m. Although we had not been attacked, we had seen plenty of further evidence of wrecks and ground fires below us. It was hard to remain unmoved when close friends might have been involved.

At debriefing, it was learned that four Upper Heyford aircraft were unreported. Later, while having our bacon and eggs, we learned one of the four had landed at a drome north of us. Our overall losses, however, were heavy at forty-eight aircraft. This was to be the last of the one thousand bomber raids for now.

A lorry dropped me off at my billet at the Manor House. We were to stand down for a day, thank goodness, because all I wanted was a few hours of sleep. I noticed two of the cots in my room were empty.

By noon I was back on my bike heading for the mess. The weather was beautiful and everything looked so calm and peaceful. My crew mates were all there for lunch. The missing crews were listed on the bulletin board, but this list was removed right after supper. Replacement crews to go on the next course would not be in for a few days. The war went on!

We were listed on the bulletin board for night flying for the next day. We would still do our eleven o'clock locals but, instead of afternoon flying training, we would switch to evening. This was really intended to help us to work as a team, but that was laid on before we went on OPS together. We did work well together. It was all a matter of confidence in the other members. That confidence was tested that evening when Bo's course took us through a balloon barrage. We hit a cable and spun around twice. The leading edges of the wings were equipped with cable cutters and, when we struck, the cable slid along the wing and dropped into a slot. This triggered a firing mechanism which drove a chisel into the cable. The cable dropped away and the balloon took off — for France, I think. It took a minute for the plane to right itself and it took an hour for the crew to do the same. This was the favourite topic of conversation in the mess for days.

My last three days at Upper Heyford were spent with three different pilots on air firing. This I enjoyed. I was leaving here with an above average rating — not that that mattered much except it gave me confidence for what lay ahead.

- CHAPTER 10 -

#83 Squadron Volunteering for Pathfinders

Just before we left on leave, we were given a pep talk by Wing Commander Mahaddy, the crew recruiter from #83 Squadron, asking if we, as a crew, would be willing to volunteer for the Pathfinder Force (P.F.F.), which was just forming. This was an elite group of crews to be trained in target marking. None of us objected, so Mahaddy told us he would arrange for our conversion training from two-engine aircraft (Wellingtons) to four-engine aircraft (Lancasters) at Scampton. Scampton, which was to be home base for #83 Squadron P.F.F., was a permanent force base in Lincolnshire. Wing Commander Hamish Mahaddy, as it turned out, was a famous, highly decorated pilot with all sorts of operations under his belt and a Scottish accent you could trip over.

I had my rail pass made out for Glasgow where I felt most at home. The other crew members were going to London. We would meet at Scampton in seven days. When I phoned Aunt Jeannie, she told me to come along by all means, and she had a surprise for me. That sure had me stymied. When I arrived at Jeannie's, she told me her surprise. Cam was there! I hadn't seen him since I left Uddingston for Stormy Downs. Aunt Jeannie explained that Cam was out for a walk with Annie, the young girl next door, and would be home soon. This gave her a chance to advise me that Cam was on a survivor's leave for two weeks and had already been there for a few days.

After supper, Cam filled me in. His crew, flying in Wimpey I.C.'s, had been on their first operation — a one thousand bomber raid to Bremen. They had engine failure, probably due to flak, and had to crash land in the North Sea about sixty miles from England. All of them had time to escape the aircraft, but had then spent four-and-a-half days in a rubber dinghy without fresh water or food. Their emergency rations had been damaged by the salt water. Finally, an aircraft from another squadron spotted them and advised the air/sea rescue team, who then picked them up. Cam also added that the pilot who spotted them came to visit and told them they were really doing a square search in hope of finding one of their own lost crews. After some hospital time, they were released as fit and then given leave before returning to operations. This was his leave!

Cam and I headed into Glasgow a few times, but not quite as energetically as we used to. I told him I had also been on the Bremen raid, and had a few scares. We didn't have to outdo each other; I think we were both a bit tired.

We went to see Scotty at her home, and her mother made us welcome. Scotty wasn't home from work yet so we just chatted with the rest of her family. Her brother, with the 51st, was healthy and enjoying his new status as a commissioned officer. I gave Scotty the two chocolate bars I had saved for her, but when her younger sister spotted them I guessed they wouldn't last long. We asked Scotty to join us for the evening at the Locarno and she seemed glad to go along. We danced a bit and I was pleased to see Cam on his feet once or twice. Cam and Scotty were quite comfortable together.

During this so called "survivor's leave," an immediate recall came through for Cam. He had to return to base at once. I didn't hear the reason for this until much later, but was stunned when I did hear. Evidently a newspaper reporter with the Toronto Telegram had arrived at the station and wanted an interview with Cameron to cover his survival in the North Sea. The station clerk was so impressed that a newspaper half-way round the world wanted to talk to him, that he forgot the reason for the leave and sent the wire telling him to return at once. Cam's next move would be to #7 Squadron at Oakington.

Before leaving Uddingston, and in the absence of Uncle John, I explained to Jeannie that I was operational now and would be less able to plan my leaves. On a squadron, the twelve crews were placed on a rotation schedule for time off of one week plus two days, a total of nine days. If losses were heavy, an airman could be back on leave again in two or three weeks until replacement crews were trained.

Our conversion only took us two weeks. We first switched from Wellingtons to Manchesters. A Manchester, for all intents and purposes, was a two-engine Lancaster, but with much less power. This only took three flights, but each of us had to review his new position on board and the pilot had to learn to fly it.

On July 21, 1942, we flew in our first Lancaster as a crew, but continued training flights for two more weeks. My own conversion, as a rear gunner, was fairly uncomplicated. Wellingtons, Manchesters and Lancs all used a Frazer Nash Turret and the only difference was mounting four machine guns instead of two — plus yards and yards of bullet tracks outside the turret. The shells fed from canisters to track and then into the turret, all automatically once the guns were cocked and the triggers pulled.

I was asked to go on OPS with other pilots while the rest of the crew continued training. One of these was as a mid-upper gunner to Osnebruk on August 10, 1942, with Pilot Officer Rayment of #83 Squadron.

- CHAPTER 11 -

#207 Squadron

As a crew, we had an important meeting with Group Captain Don Bennett and Wing Commander Mahaddy where it was decided it would be best if we had a few more operations under our belts before going on pathfinder work. A transfer to #207 Squadron was arranged. Bennett was all powerful and would eventually head up the total pathfinder effort of about six separate squadrons, including #405, a Canadian Squadron, operating as 8 Group — but that was still in the future.

Nic took to Lancasters like a duck to water, but needed a dozen short night flying sorties to become accustomed to the new controls. During that time, I did two more sorties; the first as a mid-upper gunner on August 28, to Nuremburg, and the other as a rear gunner where we dropped mines off the north-east coast of Denmark. The nickname for this type of operation was "gardening." Why, I'm not sure, except it was not considered as dangerous as high level bombing. We were fogged in at our base and diverted to Drem, in Scotland, and then flew home the next day.

My room mate at Scampton had been Glen McNichol, our pilot, which was just fine as Nic and I got along very well. This arrangement continued at Bottesford, Nottinghamshire, on #207 Squadron and, by September 13, 1942, we were back as a crew with Bremen once again as our target.

After working with four other pilots, I finally felt at ease

GENOA
207 SQUADRON
7/8 NOVEMBER 1942

F/SGT M^cNICHOL, SGT BEAUPRE, SGT CROWE,
SGT MOTT, SGT M^cFARLANE, SGT WHYTE,
SGT WILLIS, F/SGT HOBBS.

TURIN   9/10 DEC. 1942
207 SQUADRON
F/Sgt McNichol   Sgt Mott   F/Sgt Beaupre   Sgt Willis
Sgt McFarlane   Sgt Crowe   F/Sgt Hobbs
Sgt Whyte

Direct Hit awards

69

Our Operational crew 1942

George Mott (centre rear)
with our ground crew

again. Nic and I had planned our evasive action tactics, but there had been no time to plan anything with these other men.

Two more operations followed during September — one to Essen, the other to Wismar. My total to date was nine OPS, and a promotion to Flight Sergeant increased my pay a little. Nic's promotion to the same rank also came through.

On October 1, we did a long bombing trip to Wismar and again, on our return, were unable to land. We diverted to Leeming and came home the next day as soon as the fog lifted.

The next day, our crew was ordered to attend an amazing briefing. We were to train as low level bombers! We would be flying at roof-top height, one hundred Lancasters flying in formation! This was super "hush hush" for our own protection. We could talk to no one!

We practised formation flying everyday, and pub crawling every evening. In the meantime, we added new crew members. Alex Willis was a Scot who lived in Reading, England. He would become our permanent mid-upper gunner. Jack Whyte, another Scot, would become our temporary mid-under gunner. This was a new position which called for the immediate installation of a turret on the underside just in front of the bomb bay. The more the merrier!

And now, a word on the therapeutic value of oxygen! The bigger the hangover, the bigger the relief. English beer gave me a headache. However, if I was going to assist their wartime economy further, I would have to increase my intake. Oxygen made this possible. I drank my fill at night, but had to be sure I could navigate to the aircraft in the morning. Twenty feet off the ground the problem was solved; we just turned on the oxygen. With seven men drawing on the tank, the mechanic must have thought there was a hole in it.

Once more we were moved and this time to Langar, nearby and close to the City of Nottingham. The oldest pub in England was here and it was called the Trip to Jerusalem. This was a reference to the early Crusades, and the fact that the Knights in Shining Armour would gather here for their long trip to Jerusalem in search of the Holy Grail. (Now, you didn't know I was that smart, did you? If they hadn't left a brochure on the counter I wouldn't have been!)

Finally the station went on full security, and briefing was called for 7:00 p.m. We were given all the plans for flying formation on our operational height, our position in the formation and our bombing height. The target, however, was withheld. An hour later, the briefing was cancelled and we were told to stand down, but not to discuss this meeting under threat of court martial.

The next day, we did our locals and were back to ground after half-an-hour. We were told to stand down and got the O.K. to go into Nottingham, again with a warning. Two hours later, our Military Police were looking for us with instructions to return to base and report for briefing at 7:00 p.m. Since we had come in by train, we were not sure about a change of schedule and told this to the M.P. Corporal. His suggestion amused us all; stay together and finish our meal. He would call for the Paddy Wagon to come and get us. Which he did.

This time the operation was a "go" and the briefing was a long one. We would fly all the way in formation and form up over Cornwall, at which time we would drop to two hundred feet and remain there until we arrived at the target area at Le Creusot. The Schneider Works at Le Creusot manufactured ball bearings which were crucial to the German war effort. We would fly ten aircraft across the front and ten rows deep. Armour plating had been added in front of the rear gunners on #207 Squadron, and they would man the back row of the formation. Our own aircraft was given the starboard quarter position.

Take off was in the early morning and it would be two hours before we were in final formation, since these aircraft were arriving in groups from all over the Midlands. This in itself must have been a major undertaking. Once on course, we skirted France to the west until well south of St. Nazaire and continued flying very low. Instructions were to stay below two hundred feet so that radar would have difficulty spotting us. We then turned inland and from my turret I saw nothing but water below me until close to the coast, and then I saw possibly fifty fishing vessels being flattened by the prop wash of one hundred, four-engine aircraft — a most remarkable sight and not a happy one!

When we were about one hundred miles inland, the aircraft

beside us on my right (there were none on the left), lost a motor and could not maintain enough speed to keep up to the formation. This aircraft dropped back and returned by the same route we had come in to prevent being vectored and giving away our location. That would be a lonely flight back on three engines and in broad daylight. Our aircraft could not close ranks because of our corner position, which left both our starboard and port quarters exposed.

The contour of the land in this part of occupied France was made up of gently rolling farm land which we skimmed over for hours. This still took careful concentration on the part of the pilot to stay below two hundred feet.

Instructions on bombing had been handed to our crew at the last minute. The workers at the Schneider Factory were Frenchmen forced to work there by the occupying Germans. They had been secretly warned to leave the factory five minutes early and not one Frenchman was killed. The raid was a huge success. Imagine the impact of, say, ninety-five, four-engine bombers hitting a target in broad daylight from a relatively low altitude. The aircraft had stayed low until about the last twenty-five miles from the target, then climbed to a safe bombing height.

Although I watched all this with a clear view from my turret, I have forgotten how long it took for all the planes to drop their bombs. By the time our turn came to bomb, a hugh pall of smoke was rising and we were being buffeted pretty hard by the repercussions below us. You also must remember that the Lancaster carried a much bigger bomb load than the American B17's in use at that time.

Then we headed back, breaking formation and starting the long journey home in broad daylight, over enemy territory. We were on our own now, and Nic decided to hug the ground until dusk. Some tracers came up, but usually too late to hurt us. It was the fighters we worried about; they loved low flying aircraft. Once again, we were fortunate and stayed low until dusk when we climbed with about three hours of darkness ahead.

Debriefing was a champagne party that night. All the brass were there and everybody was excited. They didn't need our picture because the Mosquitos had already returned with their pictures of total destruction.

Pilot McNichol
Wireless Operator McFarlane
Bomb Aimer Crowe

The aircraft beside us that had lost an engine had arrived back in England, but crashed at the coast. It wasn't until much later that I heard their story. Once at the coast of France, they gradually increased their height and headed straight out to sea for fifty miles, and then headed north. They were spotted as a sitting duck by three Arado Biplane fighters, which were originally Italian but now German. All three attacked the Lanc in what must have been a wild battle. The rear gunner shot down one, the front gunner crippled the second and the third went home in flames after a burst from the rear guns. The Lanc had one casualty, but the rest of the crew were O.K. These men were decorated but, unfortunately, all were killed two OPS later over Germany. This was one of our #207 Squadron aircraft.

Total British losses on the raid was one aircraft!

For the past month, our crew had been going through a process of change. We would no longer use a second pilot, but would find a flight engineer to replace him. The first man who came aboard was right up our alley. He was a true Cockney from the heart of London. He was an orphan, brought up in the Barnardo Home for Boys system. He had joined the Air Force as a boy cadet and had trained as a mechanic. He was the best engine man any of us knew and highly practical during flights when things went wrong. Yes Sir, George Mott was a good man indeed and never panicked under fire. He sat beside the pilot and anticipated his needs. One trip when the perspex blew off in front of the pilot, his only comment was, "Cooee, that was close!" He then fixed up a curtain, which was a difficult task with a two hundred mile per hour wind in his face!

The next news was bad news. Bish had decided not to go P.F.F. and transferred to another squadron. Bish had been with us since the start and I missed his good natured company. With his qualifications as a navigator, he should have been in another aircraft and that is all there was to it. Another Scot, by the name of Jock Crowe, became our Bomb Aimer for a while, but eventually he became too excitable and asked for a transfer to Coastal Command. But, for the present, he was with us, stutter and all. Jock had not always stuttered, but one trip he had his target map laid out on the floor of the aircraft and he was studying it carefully as we approached the target. He lifted his head to instruct the pilot when a burst of flak from below punched a hole right through his map. After that direct hit, Jock developed his stutter!

Langar was a dispersal drome and the aircraft were parked in keys all the way around the perimeter road. Our living quarters were also dispersed, and the Aircrews lived in Nissan huts around the perimeter. There was safety in this because, from the air, we did not look like much of a target. Without a bicycle, however, you needed to be an athlete, for it must have been two miles around the perimeter, and that is a long way from the cookhouse.

We were now into a prolonged wet spell and, although the pavement dried up, the ground never did. It became a serious problem at times. If an aircraft dropped a wheel off the runway, the whole plane had to be dismantled and this happened more than once, especially with crippled planes coming in off OPS.

We had a very prim lady officer in the W.A.A.F.'s on our station who rode her bicycle with a ramrod straight back and just a modest showing of white under the hem-line. Every day she rode by at about the same time that the fire brigade were out practising. There was an on-going game of wits between the firemen and the lady officer. On one occasion, everything was working in favour of the firemen. The dew was heavy, the ground was wet and the officer was preoccupied. Up crept the fire reel until it was about ten feet behind her and then CLANG, CLANG went the big bell. The poor lady headed for the ditch. When her front wheel hit the mud beyond the asphalt the front wheel sunk, but the W.A.A.F. kept on going right over the handle bars and landed with her legs stuck in the air and all those petticoats flying. If that wasn't bad enough, every airman within fifty yards insisted on helping her. I don't know why I'm telling you this, but fifty years later I am still laughing. I think it was her stiff reserve that made it so funny.

To top everything off, the whole station was up to it's bippies in earwigs, which the English called earywiggs. The damp ground made ideal breeding grounds for earywiggs, and they responded wholeheartedly. There were earywiggs in the ditches and on the roads, above the screen doors, under the mats and even the odd hitch-hiker on board our aircraft but, above all, they were in the

Crew picture
Glen, Mac, Charlie and Bish

mess hall where they headed directly for the food warming pans and waited until we came off a late night flight. My tot of rum gave me the instant energy to chase them off my bacon, but first, I had to shovel them aside to see if it actually was bacon. All this led to another problem; we all got dysentery.

Prior to George Mott coming on board, we had pilots-in-training on board flying second position, or "second dickie" as the R.A.F. called it. Our favourite one, Sergeant Ottley, had been to the best boarding schools and spoke with an Oxford accent. The Canucks on board found this highly amusing. We didn't tease him, we just got him to talk! After some OPS experience with us, he was given his own crew and his own aircraft. We were on the tarmac to give him a send off on his first mission, where he made one circuit before coming back for a landing. Since he had a full bomb load on board, this was a very serious matter, and he was immediately put on charge. Two M.P. Sergeants came to get him and marched him into the Commanding Officer's office where a recording secretary was also seated. The charge was read out to the effect that Ottley had landed a fully bomb laden aircraft on an R.A.F. station, thereby endangering the lives of all persons nearby. The correct procedure, he was advised, was to fly the plane to the sea-shore, plug in automatic control, order everybody to bail out and send up a fighter to shoot down the aircraft.

By now, the whole station knew Ottley was in trouble. The hall outside the C.O.'s office was loaded with silent listeners. Even the two M.P's had their ears right to the door! The minute the C.O. opened his mouth, Ottley was reminded that he was in trouble indeed; the commanding officer also spoke with an Oxford accent.

"Explain your actions Ottley."

"I hardly know how to do that, Sir."

"You had better try, and fast."

Ottley had planned to explain the discomfort of an eight hour operation in badly soiled linen under his flying suit but blurted out, "I shit myself, Sir!"

"Oh," said the C.O. This was obviously not the answer he expected. "Don't do it again."

The following day, our squadron stood down and we did a

lot of lounging around. A dispersal drome did not have all the fancy conveniences of a permanent station, so they played a movie for us in the crew room which sat right on the tarmac beside the control tower. We sat on rows of dinky little benches about twelve inches deep and ten feet long — at least we were supposed to.

Our sister Lancaster squadron at Syerson was operating that day as we sat watching the movie. Suddenly, through the large window, a Lancaster came into view. Its underbelly was on fire and it dropped down fast and landed. The wheels were down and it lurched to a stop two hundred yards in front of us where the runways crossed. Out tumbled the crew and they ran in all directions. Suddenly, it dawned on us that there were bombs on board and the fifty-odd people in the room around me began to run in all directions as well. Then they tried to hide under those ridiculous little benches; rear ends up and heads down. Finally, the room was evacuated. The firemen hesitated to approach, which was just as well, since there was a "cookie" on board and the last of the crew were disappearing over a fence nearby when she exploded. The last man received considerable help from the bomb and ended up half-way across the field beyond. The bomb itself did very little damage considering it was a four thousand pounder. The difference, of course, was the fact that there was no repercussion, but she sure blew and took our plate glass window with her. All the glass in the control tower also shattered. On the crash site, there was a crater sixteen feet deep and twenty feet wide. My, what a delicious "boom" that was! I am also pleased to report that the last crew member over the fence only had a broken arm. He was presented with Glider Pilot's wings by his crew mates!

The Le Creusot raid had been my eleventh operation. That was on October 17, 1942, then it was leave time again and was I ready.

There was a very wealthy Canadian in England by the name of Lord Nuffield who made a gracious offer to all Canadian Aircrew on operations in Britain. He would pick up the total tab at any hotel during their leave in Britain. This was on-going and could be used more than once. All that was required was for the

Airman to pre-register at his own orderly office one week in advance. This made it possible to stay at the best hotels, with the best meals and the very best service. Boy, were we living! There were just the three Canadians in our crew now. Nic, Bo and I had talked it over and decided on Dundee, Scotland, because we wanted to see the Highlands but we didn't want to be too far from city lights.

To top if off, the hotel manager arranged for three sets of golf clubs, golf balls and a free pass for a beautiful course to play. Even our transportation back and forth to the course was provided. Bo was quite good, but Nic and I were duffers. I don't think there were any other players on the entire course, a situation which probably had something to do with wartime.

Back at the hotel for supper, we received some rather bold stares from high ranking naval officers for our lighthearted chatter and, I guess, that made us laugh all the more. The hotel staff responded much more warmly and, in fact, our search for dates ended right there. We loved the company, but didn't understand very much of what they said. They speak a language of their own in Dundee.

Each floor had a lounge complete with armchairs and deep chesterfields, with no need for high lighting since the hotel was almost empty. In the morning, I asked the others where they had gone to the evening before and they told me, with a grin, that they hadn't left the building. That didn't bother me since my Mabel had been a very loving companion. We must all have picked a different floor.

We wandered down the main street and stopped at a large cleaning and pressing establishment to smarten up our uniforms, since we only had one uniform each and we were wearing them. So, to accomplish this, we all had to strip off. They loaned us a room amid lots of whistles and laughter. When we came out we each had several pieces of paper in our hands with names and phone numbers that had been left in our pants pockets. We asked the girls to identify themselves, without too much success (but there was a lot of giggling).

There was a large naval establishment at Dundee, but further down the shore were all sorts of fishing boats coming in. I had

Cam and Charlie
on leave in Greenock

McNichol

McFarlane

Bishop

Beaupre

found the source of all our kippered herring! They brought in tons and salted them down. I guess over half the protein in the British diet was from fish, particularly during wartime. I have heard some very unflattering things said about kippers and Finnan Haddie in the mess halls. Mind you, in all fairness, I heard some good things about them too. They would have made good fertilizer!

Just so we didn't think we had to eat kippers to support the local economy, there was another industry in Dundee which commanded a place in world markets. That was marmalade. Thousands of people there were employed to grind up Seville oranges. I realize this is just a squirt in the bucket compared to apple juice or orange juice world-wide, but can't you just visualize those huge supply ships hurrying to unload just so that they could fill up for their return trip with Scotch whisky, marmalade and kippered herring. It does my heart good! You see, you couldn't get your hands on a bottle of Scotch there for love or money, and the marmalade all went to export. They should have been fair about it, and shipped out all the kippers!

When I returned to base, there was a letter for me from Aunt Jeannie saying she had expected to hear from Jack Cameron, but so far had not received any message. I made enquiries through Canada House and found that Cam was missing-in-action the week before. No report had yet been received from the International Red Cross. I wrote Jeannie and told her we would have to wait and see. I then wrote Mom and Dad to advise them that I knew about Cam so that they would not agonize over writing to let me know, since the Camerons were in touch with my parents whenever letters arrived.

By November 7, 1942, our crew was back on OPS and we made our first trip across the Alps to Italy. This was a nine-and-a-half hour journey and left me full of wonder. There were one hundred and seventy-five aircraft on this raid.

Our journey across France was without problems, but the moon was very bright when we skirted Switzerland. Below, by at least ten thousand feet, was a lone Whitley going around snow-capped mountains instead of over them. What an awe inspiring sight that was! Where in the world was that Whitley going?

North Africa, maybe. There were dozens of peaks below us and a total panorama of mountain-tops around us. Then the anti-aircraft guns from Switzerland opened up, firing straight up into the air. This gave the navigators a positive fix. I think this was Switzerland's way of helping us without losing their neutrality.

It took us about two hours to cross the Alps from north to south before the snow began to disappear. Visibility was excellent, the sky was dark blue and the moon cast light across the country-side. The intercom advised that there was a large metropolitan area coming up and we were close to our target. We were finally over Italy.

Most of my time then was taken up in sky searching for enemy aircraft, but none appeared. Genoa was an industrial city and the factory area was easy to see from our bombing height of eight thousand, five hundred feet. We carried two, one thousand pound bombs plus about the same weight in smaller sizes. At last the bomb aimer was locked on the target and our bombs tumbled out. Just as our bombs were falling, other aircraft appeared — all on the same course, which was reassuring. Large puffs began to appear on the ground, well grouped in the factory area.

Although the losses on Genoa had been light, two nights later we were on a six hour trip over Hamburg, where losses reached seven per cent. Unexpectedly poor weather spoiled any chance of good bombing and aircraft hung on to their bombs and went around again, when we were attacked by fighters. I think the Germans must have thought the bombs were gone, and they attacked from far too close. Some of the explosions could be felt and some fighters went down. Seldom is this action visible at night, but the clouds acted as a giant movie screen.

Again, two nights later, we were on OPS heading for Genoa, but the wiring under my feet in the turret caught fire when we were over France. All the turret control wiring was fed upward from a central column. With constant turning, the wiring may have become frayed, but there was also a pool of oil building at my feet which caught fire several times and made it hard for me to concentrate. Warm feet I didn't mind, but toasted I didn't like!

George Mott, our engineer, came back and patched it, but advised the pilot that my turret pressure would not hold up. They decided to abort the mission and we returned to base. There was danger in this — if you were spotted as a loner, the fighters were there fast. But again we were lucky.

The next morning, I phoned back to London to check on my pal, Cam. The last communique had read, "Missing, believe dead." This had now been revised to "Prisoner of war in Germany and hospitalized." This was good news, for at least he was alive. I advised Aunt Jeannie by phone at once, knowing that the Camerons would be advised by the War Office in Ottawa. It didn't pay to dwell on it, but my list of Aircrew friends was thinning out fast. I had been on operations just under six months, and over half the gunners in my course were gone.

On November 15, we took off for Genoa. That lonely, but beautiful, two hours over the Alps had a calming effect and yet, less than an hour beyond, we were over the target. During the past few operations we had a dual function: first to hang chandelier flares above the target in two opposite directions and, allowing for wind direction, then to drop our own bombs through the pattern of sky markers. The main force would then follow after one minute and again use our markers. This was the earliest form of target marking and was intended to increase the accuracy of our bombing. It would not be long before the highly trained Pathfinder Squadrons would take over this function. As it was, we were too prone to the vagaries of the winds. Our results that night were excellent, and for the first time in my memory, all seventy-eight aircraft returned to their bases safely.

One of our aircraft returning from Genoa had made an emergency landing at a fighter drome in Exeter, on the south coast of England. Minor mechanical repairs were required and our aircraft was sent there with the parts which our flight engineer could install. We had no problem getting there but, when we filed our return flight plan, we were advised that our drome, in the Midlands, was socked in with 10/10th clouds with no break in the weather foreseen. Nic requested accommodation, which was readily granted. In the mess we found all the fighter boys wanted to buy us a drink and, in fact, our other crew told us they had been in a constant state of inebriation for two days and had yet to pay for a drink. Of course, they couldn't "get home" either.

Since we had not anticipated a stop over, we had very little money with us so we asked to go on pay parade. None of us, I might add, had our pay books in our flying clothes. The pay master came over to see us and cut through all the red tape by giving each of us five pounds and asked us to sign an advance form. We were now highly mobile!

The airdrome was a busy one just a few miles outside of Exeter, close to a tiny village which had a pub and all. The Hurricanes patrolled the shore on constant alert because of the Naval Base here. It seemed there were three landing areas, two of them on wire. This dispersal system was probably in case of attack. The fields were good and firm. We ate as guests in the Officers' Mess which, in itself, was quite unusual, but on fighter dromes, speed was the name of the game. Everything else was casual. These fellows really showed respect for bomber boys and this, of course, was mutual. We couldn't get enough of their stories.

After supper we tried the local pub and were surprised to learn that they only sold rough cider. Each of us ordered a pint and found it not unpleasant, so we tried another. Alex Willis mentioned his leg had gone to sleep, and when Nic began to look a little odd and put his head down on the table we admitted to each other that it had been a long day. We decided to walk to our rooms and call it a night even if it was only about 9:30. Willis had trouble manoeuvring and Nic was almost impossible to wake up. Once outside, the fresh sea air hit us and helped to clear our heads, but it didn't help our walking much.

Back at our little hotel, there were three rooms waiting for us with two or three cots in each room. Jock Whyte put his head back on the bed but his legs came up at the knees. In one minute he was out cold and remained in that position. We were learning fast about rough cider!

The Italian raids had been quite successful to date, and Turin was added to the list on December 8, 1942. This may have been the easiest raid I was ever on and yet an aircraft seemed to explode beside us. There were no signs of flak or fighters. We bombed at six thousand feet, which was very low. The city below erupted in fires. On our return, after eight hours in the air, they advised us that all aircraft had returned regardless of what we reported.

The following night, darn it all, they sent us back again to hit Turin. We had very little rest but, although I don't remember, I imagine the moon period was involved. It was a long trip once again, but an easy trip with a minimum of flak and a complete lack of fighter aircraft. Our designated bombing height this time was four thousand, five hundred feet; the lowest ever. We did not carry four thousand pound "cookies" or twelve thousand pound "block busters" for that reason. The repercussion from those bombs would have hit us and probably would have knocked us out of control. Down below, we watched a steady stream of vehicles climbing up a mountain road. This column was miles long and every car or truck had his lights on. What an easy target that would have been, but not for us. We were after factories and utilities. Our target was quite visible and our aiming unhurried. Our return was uneventful, but scary, as morning light began to change the sky. Our crew were presented with "direct hit" reminders on these two Turin raids. This made four we had received so far.

It was leave time again and London called! Once our documents were filed with Lord Nuffield's office, we were cleared in no time and signed out for nine days. I phoned ahead to Beryl and found out she would be home in London on the weekend, so I could see her then. It was a long time since I had last seen her and I was looking forward to it — I guess I have already told you, Beryl was a beautiful girl. Well, Bo and Nic and I headed south this time and that was a change from Glasgow. We had chosen a hotel in Russell Square, which was handy to old London, and had a good meal right at the hotel because the price was right. Thanks Lord Nuffield! Even if we did have to pay for our own Whitbread ale.

Next we went to Piccadilly to the Universal Brasserie, a spot rather famous with the Canadians. If you were going to meet and lose buddies it was here — and sure enough we did. Bo met a classmate and I met a former neighbour on leave from the army. After we had been there for a couple of hours, we decided there must be more to life than drinking beer so we bought another beer and thought about it. We decided to leave off our decision till a future date because it was too important to rush into. With that,

90

we relaxed and bought a beer. The taxi driver told us it was easier to climb in one at a time. If there had been any beer handy we would have thought about that decision, too. Directions please Navigator!

The next day, we visited Canada House and had a happy talk with some real live Canadian girls. They did sound different, but then we had been away from them for over a year. Possibly they had Canadian girls on Canadian bases, but we had never been on a Canadian base in England. We ate our lunch there in the cafeteria and talked to dozens of Aircrew just arrived from back home, and all commissioned! Everyone of them was keen to get on OPS "before the war was over." We made no comment on that remark.

That evening, I was meeting Beryl with no plans other than to have supper with her locally. She was due to arrive on the train just a short bus ride from our hotel. According to her letters, her English boy friend, "whom I have known all my life," had proposed to her and she would first like to know my plans. On the job I had then I couldn't consider a long term commitment, even with a girl this lovely. I hoped she would accept this. In all honesty, my heart was with my family back home. How I would have loved to see them!

My first sight of her confirmed that she was as beautiful as I remembered her being. When she stepped off the train, my intentions wavered for a minute, but we got to the restaurant in time to order a fast drink to fortify my iron convictions. Oh brother! O.K., so I lie a little, I was a real jelly fish!

Beryl was wearing a most becoming blouse which I could not take my eyes off. It was completely fascinating. It was like watching something that might happen at any moment. How could so little support so much. She, of course, had noticed me staring and asked how I liked her new blouse. I had some prior notice on that one and promptly answered, "Tantalizingly titillating." I didn't try to build a sentence around that one since I could barely get it out as it was. She looked me straight in the eye and then began to giggle. That lightened things up a bit and I felt better. It was then I told her I could never give a long term commitment to any girl while on my present work. And, do you know, she accepted that and I felt better still. We had a wonderful evening.

A few days later, Nic, Bo and I went to Hammersmith Palace, probably the biggest dance floor in London, with alternate bands and thousands of people. Beryl joined us there, not a very good idea on my part, because Bo and Nic got more dances than I did. These guys were very tough competition, believe me. Nic was a good looking guy, about six feet tall, and Bo had the personality to make up the difference, if any. I hope they had a good time!

December was a cold, damp month with lots of down time, but we completed two more raids for the year; one to Duisberg, with two hundred and thirty-two aircraft, and the other to Munich, with one hundred and thirty-seven aircraft. Duisberg was a success but, according to reports, Munich was a failure. We lost twenty-four aircraft on these two raids alone and about one hundred and seventy airmen.

We continued with our daily locals right through till Christmas. At the same time, Bo kept being called in to secret navigational meetings. All sorts of "black boxes" were being installed in our aircraft. One was called Oboe, for blind bombing, another, called H2S, actually projected a picture of the ground below on a screen. Wow, no more blind flying! Up until now, a great deal of my time had been taken up reporting ground detail and drifts to the navigator. Before bailing out, we now had two more buttons to push!

Christmas Day that year was quiet. The British boys, of course, headed home and the rest of us went in to Nottingham and had a few drinks and a terrific steak that looked suspiciously like horse meat. We decided we were doing quite well in the survivor business, thank you very much! Since no young ladies came dashing over to our table, we headed back early. Our very own Nissan hut was not very exciting, so we hung around the mess and played penny poker for a while before finding our bikes and heading around the perimeter in the black out.

To begin the New Year, we started out for Essen, but had trouble with our new navigational equipment and were ordered to return. Of nineteen Lancs to go, three were lost. In spite of that loss, the new equipment was reported later to us as very good.

- CHAPTER 12 -

Back to #83 Squadron

In January 1943, we returned to #83 Squadron, which was now located in permanent Pathfinder Quarters at Wyton, Hunting-donshire, known as Wyton Hunts. I now had twenty operations under my belt and, once again, I had Nic as a room mate. This room was in the Sergeants' Mess and handy to both the bar and the mess hall, so we no longer had a long bike ride in the rain to get our breakfast. Both Nic and I had been promoted to Flight Sergeant just before moving here, but that was a bit of a laugh. Nearly all the Aircrew on this station were officers before they got here. The N.C.O. Mess was a big, beautiful room with no one in it. Once a month, they would stock up on new crews, but they wouldn't last. The attrition rate was very high, plus this was an R.A.F. Squadron, who looked after their own when promotions were due.

This was the month #83 Squadron was officially designated as a Pathfinder Squadron, or P.F.F. as it was called, and each Aircrew member was given a gold eagle to wear as part of his uniform. P.F.F. crews arrived over the target ahead of the main-stream of bombers and put down markers for them to bomb on. It was not long before pin-point accuracy became a possibility, and more and more damage was being done by the R.A.F. and the R.C.A.F.

#83 Squadron P.F.F. worked in conjunction with #109 Squadron, who flew Mosquitos. The "Mosy" was a relatively new

93

twin-engine aircraft capable of great speed. By that I mean it was faster than any Nazi fighter. It also flew higher than Nazi aircraft and, get this, the darn thing was made of plywood and manufactured right in Toronto! It did more than its share to win the war. Mosys didn't bother with armament — if they can't reach you, why bother carrying guns at all? They took their pictures of the potential target and brought them home just before the bombers took off, reported on the cloud cover, then went back to the target again to take pictures of the damage done by the bombers. Although the technique wasn't perfect yet, results began to improve and spirits began to lift.

#83 Squadron at Wyton was still in the middle of their organizational change and, for about three weeks, we did locals only. A dozen new faces appeared on the scene, all high ranking officers with impressive titles. Don Bennett, our C.O., had been elevated to Group Captain and was busy forming other P.F.F. Squadrons. These other squadrons, such as #405, were already in existence, but had to be fitted with the fancy new bombing "gadgets" and trained in P.F.F. techniques.

Our mess began to fill up again. When George Bishop left our crew, an experienced Bomb Aimer was brought on board to fly with us permanently. After our interim experience with Jock Crowe, Bill Lewis was a winner and fitted in very well. Lewis, an American from Ohio, had a Distinguished Flying Cross on his jacket and a few good tales to tell. My favourite one had him bailing out over the highlands, living with a crofter, and drinking whisky for a few weeks before he reported back. And then there was his English girl friend, Penelope, in London...

We attended briefing again on January 23, 1943. Our target would be Lorient, the French submarine base. The Germans had literally buried this crucial base in tons of concrete, constructing it so well that bombers had not been able to reach it. Our new 6 Group now had a job to do, since submarines were devastating the Merchant Navy.

We kept going back. The next one was on the January 26, but the weather was wrong.

The following night, we were over Dusseldorf and, for the first time, would use our new bombing techniques. A Mosquito
94

using the new "oboe equipment" found the target and dropped a target indicator, or ground marker. Then along came the Pathfinder Force and reinforced this indicator several times with colours before the main bomber force came in. This proved very successful.

On February 1, 1943, we did a night flying test which was not what I had in mind for my twenty-second birthday celebration. The following two nights we were on OPS to Cologne and Hamburg, and each time we carried four thousand pound "cookies."

Our activities were stepped up now, concentrating on the sea ports and submarine bases at Lorient, Wilhelmshaven and Bremen, where we went back time and time again, and another trip to Milan, Italy for good measure. My total OPS was now over thirty. Our losses had been very heavy, the mess was getting lonely again and, just to add to our problems, the bulletin board announced our very own Harold Henry Jean de Beaupre — "Bo" — was now a Pilot Officer. The promotion I didn't mind, but why did they have to muck up our bridge games? Bo had earned every bit of this, by the way. Nic had also earned a promotion, but there was no sign of it as yet. There never was a better bomber pilot and nobody knows better than the rear gunner who feels everything times ten!

At the end of February, 1943, Bo moved to the Officers' Mess, joining Bill Lewis, who was already there.

Our rotation leaves were coming up so fast that once or twice I didn't go. Even with Lord Nuffield standing by, it cost more than I was making, but this time Nic suggested the four of us go to Glasgow and use Lord Nuffield's scheme. When Bo and Bill Lewis were reached, they agreed to the plan. I intended to go out to see Jeannie regardless. Bo made the arrangements and Mac was pleased we were going to Glasgow, even suggesting the best hotel for us. The other crew members headed home, as usual.

We arrived during the second week in February and I immediately headed out to see Aunt Jeannie and Captain John McColl. They were both at home and, although it was good to see them, they both avoided discussing Cam until I brought the subject up. Down for the second time, the man they looked upon as a son had bailed out and landed in Germany, where he had been hospitalized and taken prisoner. I explained to them my feelings, and told them that losses were so high on operations that his situation was actually good news. His foot was badly banged up but, otherwise, he was O.K. and this was a blessing, because with any luck he would return home after the war. The teapot took a real beating that day! We talked for hours. I learned that Ian was away again, but doing fine, and, according to Johnny, he handled his new job as Captain easily. Captain John, on the other hand, was well into his seventies and was up for retirement for the second time. He would do his last Dublin to Glasgow run at the end of the month. When I had supper at Uddingston and then headed back to the hotel, Jeannie understood. God bless her!

Our boys were still eating in the dining room when I returned and wanted to know why I hadn't told them about this place before. I told them they just couldn't afford it. Thank you again, Lord Nuffield. These colonials just didn't know the best places, did they?

I phoned Scotty, but when I missed her and talked to her little sister, she let it out of the bag that Scotty was on a date. This I really didn't mind because, here again, I did not want firm commitments. It also gave me a chance to tease her! I left a message for Scotty to meet me for lunch, if possible, the next day.

The four of us did our drinking at the hotel bar that evening. We had diverse plans for the following day, and we arranged to meet at the Locarno the following evening. Since the weather was miserable that night, it was just as well we stayed in. Sleep was no problem!

Scotty showed up the next day, as I had hoped she would, and the weather had finally cleared. What more could a clean-cut, young Canadian lad ask for? It was Saturday, so we just wandered around the stores and then went to lunch, completely at ease with each other. It was still fun for me to sit back and listen to the accent. A movie filled in our afternoon and fish and chips in the park was our supper menu. We joined the others, including Mac and his pretty wife, at the Locarno. We were a party of seven and you know what that meant with these guys! Occasionally I was able to break in and see that Scotty was all right. I regret to say that she admitted to being all right; in fact she said she loved it.

96

I had a dance with Mac's wife and asked her how to handle this situation, but she just laughed and said "grin and bear it." This young mother was a beautiful dancer herself and didn't seem to mind Mac flying with wild men, so I was not suffering altogether. When she asked how Mac was doing on the job, I promptly told her if he continued in his present mould, we would take him in permanently, but he still hadn't learned Canadian. I think each member of the crew, in turn, had kidded her along, and she seemed to thrive on it. She was positively radiant.

The next morning I was off again to Uddingston for a final visit with Jeannie. This wonderful lady knew from experience with her own family not to anticipate the future; to take it a day at a time. She did, however, ask how many times I had "flown against the Enemy." When I told her over thirty times, that was the end of that conversation. She went to the cupboard and brought out a can of Devon Cream, a spoon and a can opener. Do you know, I spooned the whole thing. You just couldn't buy that kind of a treat! Once more, I went into the "living room" to admire the elephants. There was an addition or two and, my goodness, the sheen of the ebony was beautiful.

Two days later, we were on the train again heading for Edinburgh, then Nottingham, then on to our home base at Wyton in Huntingdonshire.

We still had one day left on our leave when we returned, and that day was an important reminder that the war hadn't stopped because we were on leave. Two medium sized raids had been carried out in our absence, and several of our aircraft from Wyton had failed to return. We tried to identify the men involved, but couldn't. We were beginning again to feel like strangers on our own drome, especially with Bo and Lewis in the other mess.

When I walked out to the edge of the tarmac, a pleasant surprise awaited me. Sitting there was a Hurricane Fighter plane, whose pilot came towards me and asked where the Sergeant's Mess was located. We both laughed when we realized that the pilot, Bill Gunn, was a class-mate of mine from high school. We returned to the mess to have a beer together. Bill had been a highly respected athlete at Jarvis Collegiate in nearly every sport. He was engaged or had an understanding with a lovely former neighbour of mine by the name of Marg Niddery, who was nursing at Christie Street Hospital. While attached to the R.A.F. doing recognisance in the north of Scotland, he said he had been dying of boredom, but his request for a transfer had finally come through, so he was now in transit to India. This chance meeting had cheered me up no end. It saddened me when I returned home years later to learn that Bill had been lost in action.

We gave our Lanc a very good going over on our return, to be sure nothing had been overlooked. These aircraft were in constant use and seldom got the chance to become very old. The average Lanc and crew lasted six operations — although that figure was never quoted to us at the time.

Our first target back on the job was a return to St. Nazaire, but this time with a much bigger force. We seemed to plaster the dock areas pretty well and only one aircraft was lost on the morning report.

We looked forward to the entertainment provided by a troop of entertainers that came around every few months to put on a show for us. Because the shows were good, the building would be packed with all ranks. In fact, there were so many high ranking officers in attendance it barely left room for the other ranks. This was not what it was supposed to be all about and the following address by the top brass was not what it was all about either:

"Officers and their Ladies,
N.C.O's and their Wives,
Men and their Women!"

If this had been the opening of a speech in Canada, the speaker would have been lynched.

These shows were run by an organization called the E.N.S.A., and were well known by all the troops in England. After each show, it was customary for the troop to retire to the N.C.O. Mess for a drink, and it was customary for the mess to pay for that round. But, once again, there were practically no N.C.O.'s on the station. A panic call was made to the Officers' Mess. I don't remember the outcome. I had enough and went to my room.

My thirty-fourth and thirty-fifth operations were over Berlin, which was new territory for us. We anticipated problems, being so deep into Nazi Germany, and, at Briefing, they warned us that the defences were heavy and to stay above twenty thousand feet, due to heavy flak concentrations. On the first of these raids, the weather was against us and our new target finding equipment, which relied a great deal on timing, was thrown off when the bombers did not arrive on schedule, due to the winds. Damage to Berlin was light, but there was a cow pasture fifteen miles away that took one helluva licking.

The second raid on Berlin three days later was a little more successful, but much more difficult. The aircraft were icing up, which could be a very treacherous condition. A layer of ice would build up on the leading edge of the wing and change the flight dynamics of the aircraft. Sometimes the sheer weight of the ice forced a plane down. This could sometimes be treated mechanically, or chemically, in flight, but then there was no time for anything else so the bombing accuracy suffered. Twenty-one aircraft evidently were lost that day — that adds up to one hundred and fifty Aircrew. Once again, it was a long journey home with fighters all around, but we were able to see them first and turn sharply towards them, a manoeuvre that shortened the time a fighter needed to line up his sights. At night, you could lose a fighter in one pass, and then hope he didn't find you again, since vision on a dark night was limited to about three hundred yards.

We spotted many burning aircraft, both in the air and on the ground, leaving me more than ready for my rum ration. Debriefing had taken quite a while because there was much to report. We gave as much information on locations of burning aircraft as possible, as well as bomb damage at the target. We also reported on fighter action and sightings. Bring on the bacon and eggs! It was three in the morning and the rum had given me an appetite.

Although I did not realize it at the time, on April 4, 1942, we were fast becoming part of a legend. The aircraft we took up for testing that morning had just returned from inspection. It was Lancaster #R5868 Q (for Queenie). The next day, we flew Queenie to St. Nazaire on a bombing mission and returned after a successful raid. A small idea of our continuing progress is determined by the fact that both St. Nazaire and Lorient were then removed from the list of enemy targets to be attacked. And Queenie went on to become the longest survivor of the war and today, fifty years later, she is on display at Hendon, England. She recorded one hundred and thirty-seven operations and she flew on OPS from 1942 until the end of the war.

These aircraft needed constant servicing, due to the beating they took, so, while out of service, the regular crew assigned to Queenie would draw another aircraft from the pool until she returned. Over the years, no less than a dozen aircraft were lost while waiting for Queenie, but she flew on and on. Again, I would remind you that the average life of a Lancaster was six operations.

On April 3, we hit Essen with a large force of aircraft. It was very successful and two hundred and twenty-five of the three hundred and forty-eight planes were Lancasters. This was the largest force of Lancasters assembled so far and, of course, with our loss rate climbing, it was not easy to build a reserve of these wonderful aircraft. Twenty-one aircraft were lost on that mission.

On April 4, it was Kiel, with even heavier force, but poor results. This was our crew's third night of operations in a row. Twelve aircraft were lost.

I was pleased when our pilot, Glen McNichol's, name appeared on the bulletin board advising that the R.A.F. had granted his commission. I felt that it should have been done a year before that.

Just to keep things in perspective for the reader, although there were raids going on nearly everyday that weather permitted, no one squadron went on all of them. It took time to regroup after losses. We went when we were called. No one on our crew ever reported sick; hungover maybe, but never sick. But so many were not coming back at all.

We took a week's leave in London to celebrate Nic's promotion and allow time to be outfitted with new everything. He was one good looking dude, but we didn't tell him that!

As the only remaining R.C.A.F., non-commissioned officer in the mess, I expected to be very lonely unless there were some coming in on the next draft. There seemed to be no end of Canadian Aircrew volunteers, but these men now had to have some operational experience on other bomber squadrons to be chosen as Pathfinders. Then they would try to get on a Canadian Pathfinder Squadron, such as #405, as a first choice. (Better grub! No kippers!)

We went the rounds of our usual haunts while in London and I must admit we let off a lot of steam. Just after tanking up at the Universal Brasserie, we were approached from behind by a middle-aged dolly who hooked her arm through ours and asked if we would like a sporting woman. This was a stock phrase in this district and guess what we did? Wrong! We didn't, but we had a good laugh.

We went to the matinee at the Windmill Theatre because Bill's girlfriend was supposed to be in the chorus line. The Windmill was famous for its scantily dressed dancers who were advertised on the marquee as nude. This was not quite true. The law allowed for nudity — but not in motion — so, while the chorus girls were dancing their little hearts out with nobody noticing, six girls in the background were standing in various poses without moving. They were nude and they were noticed. The baldheaded row were all there up front, as usual, but the Air Force sat right behind them. Quite a show! This part of the entertainment hadn't changed for years, but we didn't care.

While in the district, I found the commercial address of my Mother's brother, Jim Black, who ran an interesting business. He held world patents on a method he had invented for printing plate manufacture on curved surfaces or cylinders by using electrolysis. When he invited me to supper on Sunday and suggested I "bring a friend," I fooled him by bringing Nic. Jim promptly lined up a dinner companion for me and Nic took my cousin Mary, a good kid about two years older than I was. Nic must have made quite an impression because I kept getting mail from Mary wanting to know how Nic was.

That was the night of the yellow fog, the most relentless and stifling fog I had ever known. There were men at the bus stops using loud speakers to tell people to get inside. We were in Sussex, eighteen miles from downtown London, and we could barely see our hands in front of our faces. How we got home I will never know.

When we returned to Wyton, Mac was already back from

Glasgow and I asked him how many new men he had seen. "Not many in our mess," was his answer. Translated into layman's language, this meant that all the new pilots and observers were officers and would use the Officers' Mess. There were some Canadian Gunners, so I wandered around to meet them. They had all graduated from 1942 classes, and most had done about ten OPS. They knew the score and had already lost over half their class-mates, so I didn't hear the same bravado I usually heard from the new recruits on a regular squadron.

On April 13, 1943, we flew on a nine-hour trip to Spezia in Italy, with an option to land in North Africa if in difficulty. We carried a big nasty bomb with a pressure sensitive fuse to explode above the harbour. It did explode above the water, which made us very happy because a hang-up meant an early bail out — four hours early!

The following night it was Stuttgart. Another long trip of seven-and-a-half hours, with twenty-three aircraft lost.

My operational trip total was now in the forties, with clarification needed on an additional two. We had signed a contract with #83 Squadron to do forty-five operations without a long break between a first tour of thirty and a second tour of fifteen. Each member of the crew had a different total, due to time off for special training courses and Pilot, Navigator conversion to four-engine aircraft. I had turned down a gunnery leader course just two weeks before for this very reason; two more operations and I would probably be finished. I tried not to dwell too much on that fact, but it was very unsettling!

- CHAPTER 13 -

Close to the Finish
#83 Squadron

Two raids were planned for the night of April 16 and 17, and our briefing covered both of them, since they were on a course near to each other. Our own target was a ten hour trip to the Skoda Works at Pilsen in Czechoslovakia. The other was on Manheim. I believe the idea was to make the Nazis think our target was Manheim, then we would go right past to Pilsen. Over fifty aircraft were lost — and our aircraft was one of those casualties.

We flew a seven man crew. Our Pilot was Pilot Officer Glen McNichol with Sergeant George Mott sitting beside him as flight engineer. Pilot Officer Bill Lewis, our bomb aimer, was up forward in the nose, and Pilot Officer Harold Beaupre of Waterloo was our Navigator. Both Lewis and Beaupre wore the Observer Wing, which qualified them for bomb aimer or navigator. Sergeant Stan MacFarlane had been with us from the start as our Wireless Operator. Sergeant Alex Willis had a good number of operations with us by now as our Mid Upper Gunner. And that just leaves Flight Sergeant Charles "Hobby" Hobbs as Rear Gunner.

All of us were on good terms and hoping for the best on what we knew would be our last flight together as a crew. Under normal circumstances, once the crew was settled in, I closed my turret doors and didn't see them until we returned. I had two methods of reaching the pilot: the first was over the intercom, but if this was out of commission there were two coloured buttons by my side. The red one signalled a turn to starboard and the green one a turn to port. In the air, I did not see any of the aircraft behind my turret. Just the tips of the tail assembly were visible above the aircraft. When I looked out, I experienced a very exposed feeling of loneliness.

We flew to the target in bright moonlight; too bright really because our own aircraft was casting shadows that looked like huge photographs, they were so clear. However, our trip inward was uneventful. There were aircraft nearby, but nothing that was threatening. When we were getting near the target and had been in transit for over four hours, Lewis reported bombing activity ahead.

During the bombing run, I couldn't see forward for a full minute while the aircraft was held steady. This was always a terrifying minute while I tried hard to see everything out back at once. Then it was "bombs gone" and we headed out like a scared rabbit, diving and weaving and turning for home. We had bombed from six thousand feet, which was quite low, so Nic kept us low for the next half hour. We could see Manheim off to the side taking a real beating when suddenly a battery of searchlights, out of nowhere, caught us and hung on. By this time, we were "roof topping" as low as we dared to avoid the lights and flak, but we were hit several times and one motor cut out. I opened up with four Brownings, trying to knock out the batteries below, when Nic said we would have to climb to maintain height for the long trip home. Ten minutes later, the second motor on the starboard side started to give us trouble and caught fire. The engine was feathered and flooded to put out the fire. Fortunately, this strategy worked. We didn't want to "dive" it out because we were now down to two engines, both on one side, which affected our manoeuvrability.

A Lancaster flew well on two engines, but gaining height was a slow process, one we had been through before. We were well into France when the third motor conked out — the motor that supplied Hydraulic power to my gun turret. The intercom was also gone, so Bo came back to warn me that a decision had been made to bail out and told me to come forward. As I climbed
104

forward I could see plenty of damage all around me. Willis had been hit and couldn't bail out.

By the time I got half-way forward, a fighter hit us with cannon shells. The others were all bailing out, except Nic who was holding the plane steady. I stood beside him for a moment, then told him I would see if the fires out back could be put out. When I returned with the news that they could not, he asked me to unbuckle his parachute since we were now too low to bail out. The only suggestion I could make was to head for water, then stood beside his seat with my arm across the back of his chair. There was no water in sight yet, so I knew we must still be well inland.

Just then the fighter came in again and shot the controls out of Nic's hands. The nose came up and then straight down, and Nic was killed.

When I came to, we were on the ground. I saw Willis with his foot trapped in the rubble and tried to help him, but my arms were not working. I told him I would be back, then walked one hundred yards with the vague idea of escaping later. I realized at that moment I was helpless.

A young boy was watching me, so I kept walking, and he followed me until I turned into the trees. He was Dutch, but he spoke some English, so I got him to remove my parachute and hide it along with my moccasin type boots and my coveralls. I then went back to help Willis but, by this time, he had been able to extricate himself.

We had crashed in German occupied France and the boy had been afraid to go near the wreck because of the Germans.

I did not know at the time that our plane crash had been photographed by a Dutch slave worker, who subsequently found my name inside my flying boots that the boy had removed. These photographs were in excellent condition and were sent to me after the war. The photographer had traced me through the R.A.F. records office in London. This man would have been shot by the Germans if he was caught with a camera!

I was pretty badly scratched up and pieces of shrapnel from the fighter's shells had pierced my hip. I was relieved to find a house nearby, and more than pleased to find some of the crew

This series of seven pictures are all of the aircraft
when it crashed at Pont À Vert near Rheims in France.

Same crash site 50 years later

who had bailed out gathered inside. They were a sorry looking lot with broken bones and make-shift bandages. Each of them needed first aid pretty badly. All I cared about, for the moment, was some warm water and a cloth, which was supplied to me by the woman of the house. Just then, the Germans arrived and soldiers began threatening us with bayonets. Not a very friendly way to treat strangers! They searched us and marched us outside, where a German Air Force officer, who spoke perfect English, was waiting. He asked for our "parole," by which he meant if we gave our word we would not try to escape he would take us for first aid. He sat beside his driver and packed us into the back, then they drove us to the airdrome for first aid. It was then that I noticed Bill Lewis was missing. From his position in the aircraft I knew he would have been the first man out which could have meant that he was miles away when he landed. What sort of shape he was in nobody knew.

While they were removing the steel slivers from my hip, the Pilot who had shot us down came over to find out why I had not used my guns. This was tough for me to answer without profanity, but then I realized he was just doing a job. I noticed he was much older than we were. The ground crew were busy congratulating him, although it was surely not much of a prize to have knocked out a cripple.

They drove us to Rheims to the American Memorial Hospital, which had been donated to France by the Americans following World War I, but was now in German hands. Some of the nurses were German, but all the support staff were French. They tried hard to show their affection, but had to be so very careful. For all intents and purposes, they were slaves.

They took us first to an X-ray room and told us all to strip off, with no regard for privacy. The German nurses were laughing and the guards were barking, but one of the French nurses was crying as everybody stood around us. There was a large horizontal X-ray table and each one of us sat down on this in turn. Although it was only about one inch too high to climb up on, my arms would not lift me, so it was my turn to be laughed at. Finally, one big horse of a girl picked me up and dropped me on the table, which made me feel even worse.

We were then all taken to one ward with barred windows, where the French girls did the nursing. They were very kind and did everything they could to care for us.

After a few days, some of us could be moved to a guarded holding unit awaiting orders as to our disposition. This turned out to be a big home converted to offices on the first floor and cells on the second floor, with bars on the windows and guards patrolling the perimeter of the building. They had gathered about twenty of us in the past few days and would make up a convoy of us any day now. It was here I met my first Canadian P.O.W., Stu Murray from Stellarton, Nova Scotia. His arm had been badly shot up and he had been in hospital for sometime. He was the one that told me how lucky we were to have been picked up by the Luftwaffe rather than the Gestapo (National Security Police), who were a proper bunch of bastards.

The bars on the windows interested me because they had been fitted into tight fitting frames with no nails showing. The bars dropped into slots just below the sill and held the frame so that it could not be pulled out. Clever construction, but with one weakness: the bottom sill was concrete on stone but the top was plaster. I had a plan!

For the first half hour, I worked on the bars. There was not enough up and down stomping space, but then some plaster dust began to filter down. Gradually each upstroke would yield a little more; at first a sixteenth of an inch and then an eighth. I had to continuously pick up the plaster dust and shake it out the window. When a quarter inch of play was available I could really thump it, but had to consider the noise. After another hour, the bar came free, then I carefully replaced it. I talked to all the others about the possibility of escape, but they were bandaged up pretty well and couldn't join me. I began to feel very lonely contemplating doing it alone. I sat down beside Stu to discuss my plan. He, of course, could not join me, but he offered me his shoes, since I only had electric cloth slippers with the wires pulled off. I decided to try, but I had to wait until dark.

After our evening food ration was served, some of the boys helped me knot sheets together and tie one end to the iron bar which would sit sideways in the frame. The drop was not too far,

112

so the sheets would take me within seven or eight feet of the ground, while the knots would make a good hand grip. I had to turn my back to wedge through the window space, then started down as quietly as I could. When I looked down, there was a German guard with a gun and a dog, and my whole system froze in fear. He hadn't spotted me yet, so I started back up, hand over hand, as fast as I could. I was just off the sill when he shouted. I think he was so startled he did nothing. One of the boys above reached me and hauled me in fast, the knots came out and the bar went back in but, strangely enough, nobody came to assist the guard. They must have all left for the day.

The next morning we were moved. The Germans gave us travel food, which consisted of three inches of coarse sausage, two inches in diameter, a piece of margarine and a quarter loaf of bread. We were warned this was to do us for two days. Then an open lorry drove us to the rail station. The German soldiers cut and spread their bread with a bayonet. What we were supposed to do we didn't know yet, nor did we know what to carry it in. However, we learned a great deal as we travelled. Our best source of information was from other prisoners when they could talk without being noticed. We discovered that many Europeans had at least a few words of English.

All able bodied men in occupied Europe were taken from their homes and shipped out of their own country, as either slave workers or soldiers. They had no other personal option but death — they fought for the Nazis or they slaved for the Nazis! Any one of them caught talking to us got the rifle butt.

There were strange sights for us to see as the truck moved along. Never had we seen old women shovelling coal into box-cars or crippled men pushing loaded carts. We finally pulled into a subway station on the outskirts of Paris and were put on board, again under guard. This train evidently took us across the city.

- CHAPTER 14 -

A Prisoner of War

We were being shipped to Frankfurt-on-Main for interrogation, to a prison camp called Dulag Luft, designated "Luft" for Air Force, as opposed to Army or Navy. We had been warned in England about Dulag Luft and its interrogation methods. Our instructions, if captured, had been clear; we were to give only our names, numbers and ranks! We had been given no additional instructions to follow when faced with threats, abuse or starvation.

We had a long train trip ahead of us, from Paris into the heart of Germany. We were given mugs of black coffee at the station and were told there would be no more for about ten hours. No change of clothing had been offered, so I still did not have shoes. Finally, we were loaded onto the crowded train. Three of us were in my compartment, plus the guard, one civilian and a German officer. When the officer first entered, George Mott's feet were stuck out and, sure enough, the officer stumbled over them. He literally screamed at Mott to remove his feet. Mott, whom I knew from before as fearless, told him to go f—- himself. The officer drew his revolver and aimed it at George, who withdrew his feet slowly while all the time looking directly into the officer's eyes. Fortunately, it was the young officer who backed off. "George," I thought, "would you mind sitting on the other side next time?"

It was late the second day when we finally saw the station signs for Frankfurt, where we disembarked and were lined up on the platform to be counted. Since we had arrived, I didn't think I would need what was left of my dried up loaf and tossed it under the train. That was a mistake! In nothing flat, there was a scramble of people after those crusts, labourers who were working near us. The nearest German said, "You shouldn't have done that, they will kill for food." I responded, "Doesn't the Master Race feed these people?" He didn't answer. I was learning!

To go from our form of freedom to this existence was difficult for me to absorb.

Half an hour later, we were at Dulag Luft. It was easy to recognize because of the barbed wire enclosure and the posten boxes, but the building we were marched into was long, narrow and low. This turned out to be the interrogation building.

Each one of us was put in a small cell and told to remove our clothing. Then, one at a time, we were taken across the hall and dusted for lice, permitted to use the lavatory, then returned to our cells. Our clothes would be returned after fumigation. The cell could not have been much more than eight feet by twelve feet, if that. There was a cot, a small table and chair, and a window too high for me to see out of. The door had a peep hole, a food slot, a light bulb above and a button to call the guard if you needed to go to the toilet. There was no washstand. There was a blunt knife, a large spoon, a small wash basin and a water jug. The light bulb was out of reach and there was no switch, so the light stayed on! The room was hot and there was no control or ventilation. Welcome home!

Meals were more than a change, they were a disaster. For lunch I had a boiled potato in it's skin, one section of bread to do me all day, some margarine, and ersatz coffee made from roasted wheat. The bread tasted like sawdust, only heavier, the coffee tasted like burnt toast and the margarine tasted like shit. The food was going to take a little getting used to — I was beginning to miss those kippers. When the guard informed me that the margarine was made from coal, it was the first time I ever believed a German. For supper, I got another potato and a bowl of spinach with a hunk of margarine on top. The spinach was a special consideration from Adolf Hitler for his birthday, so after supper I sent my condolences and a bowl of spinach to the guard, a gesture which left me pretty hungry.

By two in the morning, I was suffering from night starvation. As a young man, this is not what I thought that expression meant at all!

About 8:00 a.m., the guard asked if I wanted to use the washroom and gave me five minutes. I was permitted no contact with any other P.O.W. At 8:30 a.m., my tray arrived, containing a section of black bread equal to about three slices, a mug of coffee and a spoonful of jam made from hawberries. That was it, and the bread was meant to last all day!

They left me alone for two days to make me nervous, and the tactic worked. When my clothes, such as they were, came back to me from the laundry, they were wrinkled, but clean. My socks were not quite as long as they had been two days before, but I felt a little more sure of myself with something on. By this time, I had become so acclimatized to my nakedness, I figured I might have a future on the stage at the Roxy.

A blond German with remarkable eyes came to visit me. There was no apparent pupil to his eyes, just sea-blue colour. He was full of good humour and camaraderie and announced himself as being the representative from the International Red Cross. He wore an arm band with the Red Cross symbol on it and told me he would notify my family at once and tell them I was alive. All I had to do was fill out the form he would leave with me giving him the required information about myself. He would pick it up the next day. I glanced at the form, gave it back to him, and said, "My name is Charles Hobbs, Flight Sergeant, R85583." The printed form asked for information about my Squadron number and location, what type of aircraft flown, and more.

He immediately got angry and told me if I did not co-operate my family might never know my fate, and how could he help me if he didn't even know my name? I told him I was sorry I could give no further information. This was an unnerving experience; there I was, on my own in a foreign land in enemy hands, and just into my twenty-second year. I was terrified.

The next morning, another man in a suit came in to see me and, first off, he offered me a cigarette. A Chesterfield, no less! He was older but smoother, and nagged at me for quite a while, but I doubt if he got much from our conversation. He left two cigarettes for me in the package when he departed and a mild warning that some of the other men who would be in to see me, especially the Gestapo, were notorious for using stronger methods than he did. His parting words did nothing to make me rest easier. I lit a cigarette with the match folder he left, and it made my head swim. I had not had a smoke for a week.

Two days later, in came my blue-eyed friend, but this time the pretence was gone. He was in the Nazi officer's uniform of the Luftwaffe and, for all I was mad as hell at them, I still had to admire that uniform. Each one of them must have had a private tailor!

It would seem they were having difficulty identifying my pilot and needed my help. I held tough. My blue-eyed "little temper" now became my blue-eyed "Big Temper." He was having a real tantrum for sure! I offered to call for a glass of water, but this only made him worse. In the meantime, I was making sure I kept the table between us. Finally, he simmered down and departed. I never saw him again.

It was a long, boring week before anyone came back to see me and, sure enough, this one must have been the Gestapo with his black, knee length leather coat and dark fedora with the brim down on all sides. He looked right out of a Hollywood movie. He opened his coat to be sure I saw his oversized revolver, a Colt probably, and went through one of their routines, fully rehearsed. The trouble was, I didn't know it was a routine.

"Who is your Pilot?"

"My name is ..."

"What kind of aircraft? You don't have to tell me, we know everything."

"My name is Charlie."

Just then there was a shot from down the hall. "That's your neighbour who refused to co-operate. He was warned. Do you want the same thing?"

"My name is ..."

Exit one Gestapo. I hoped the little brown spots didn't show!

I was in solitary for sixteen days. My stomach had begun to shrink, but I was still hungry all the time. That morning, the guard asked me if I wanted a shave. Yes, I wanted a shave. I had been sixteen days without shaving and, although I didn't have a heavy beard, it was all over and felt dirty. He handed me a safety razor with a second-hand blade, but no soft soap. Just a cake of hard, grey stuff that looked very like a bar of Snap hand cleaner. It was nearly impossible to create a lather, but I rubbed it on anyway and started in. The blade was dull as hell and I went back over it a few times, but there were too many nicks. I removed the blade and honed it on my upper thumb. It worked a little better, but eventually I gave up. Warm water would have helped!

Later that morning, the older interrogator came back and told me that all the information they needed was now in their hands and he showed me the cover of a file. He asked me if I wanted him to read it and I said, "If you like," then turned away to listen in case any surprises showed on my face.

"Your pilot's name was Bren McNichol. He was killed. Your Halifax came down in flames." I was glad I wasn't looking at him, since the pilot's name was Glen and we had flown a Lancaster and not a Halifax. Then it dawned on me that these were just traps. All I said was "Thank you." He smiled as he told me the name of my Commanding Officer and Station.

I was now told I would be moved to the compound where my friends were and, that afternoon, I did go on clothing parade for wooden shoes and then finally into the sunlight. There was a large compound, or field, surrounded by double rows of barbed wire with rolls of barbed wire inside that. A single strand of warning wire sat six feet inside, supported by low posts. I recall that there were six posten boxes, each with two machine-guns sitting high above the fences.

When the gates opened to let me through, I was immediately met by a Canadian Sergeant who told me to keep my mouth shut unless I knew who I was talking to. He told me there were listening devices and people under the roof above the bunks. He reminded me that this was still an interrogation camp.

The new arrivals went on parade and each of us received a Red Cross food parcel. These parcels were supplied by several different countries, but these particular ones were from Canada, as a large percentage of them were. A ten pound parcel was a beauty to behold: hard tack biscuits, a tin of jam, three cans of meat, a pound tin of Maple Leaf butter, a tin of Klim milk powder, a compressed tin of rolled oats to be cooked, a tin of cheese, two chocolate bars and two packs of twenty-five cigarettes. At the moment, the cigarettes were the most important item there! Everything stopped while we lit up. We found we could take quite a beating providing we had a smoke.

One slice of bread, margarine and a cooked potato were supplied with each meal at this camp, and some thin cabbage soup with nothing in it but cabbage. We supplemented this, of course, with our food parcels.

There were two of my crew here now, George Mott and Stan MacFarlane. I was glad to see Stan again and I wondered if his wife had received the good news yet that he was alive, since mail evidently took a long time to get through. There were some British Army boys, who worked here, and they gave us some information. We watched them pretty carefully in case they were Gerrys too. We were well aware that, before the war, there was an easy exchange of nationalities across Europe until Hitler messed it up. A Gerry could easily have passed for an Englishman except in Yorkshire, where they have a language all their own.

We did not have the pots and pans yet to make the most of our Red Cross food. Our tin plates were collected after each meal. The British Army boys who worked here for the Germans did the cooking. They were prisoners of war and considered themselves lucky to be here rather than in the salt mines. That, I do believe, but never did figure out how they had been selected.

Each day I watched the gate for men I might recognize among the dozen a day coming in, but had had no luck so far. The large numbers of new prisoners were not a good sign.

Within a few days, I found a boy who was willing to trade an old pair of shoes for a pound of butter. The shoes were not too small, so he got his tin of butter. Too big I could fix, but too small I couldn't!

- CHAPTER 15 -

From Dulag to Barth by Cattlecar

One night we were told to pack up and prepare for moving in the morning. That wouldn't take very long, since I didn't even have a tooth brush. I decided to take the clogs with me in case my recent purchase turned out not to have too many miles left in them.

I know there must have been at least forty of us because, when the lorries arrived at the railway, they packed forty of us, plus an armed guard, into one boxcar. For sanitation there was one two gallon pail, so we assumed we would be stopping often. Boy, were we wrong! We were on board for five days with only one stop where we were allowed out at the side of a field. The guards formed a semi-circle to keep us confined. There is a spot there where the rhubarb was plentiful for years to come.

Then began one of the most fascinating episodes of my life to date. The guard who was locked in our car carried a rifle and bayonet, although the bayonet was in its scabbard. He was a decent sort who spoke a little English, a First World War vet who closely resembled one of our home guards. He sat down on the straw covered floor near us and put down his rifle, succumbing to the friendship of our boys.

Each of us had most of a Red Cross parcel left, plus our travel ration of a half a loaf of black bread, margarine, a small round of horse meat sausage, coffee and water containers of all sorts including old tin cans. We made up a large hard tack (dog biscuit was our name for it) with real butter on it and real jam and gave it to the guard who didn't believe his eyes. He looked at it, smelled it and licked at it long enough for one of our boys to remove the rifle bullets from his gun. Someone handed another biscuit to him. Then first one, then another, of the boys asked to borrow the bayonet to cut his sausage. This type of fast action was so new to me I was having difficulty in following everything myself. The bayonet was forwarded quickly to the far end of the car where two New Zealanders had found a split floor board and were busy cutting through it. The guard did enquire about his bayonet but was told not to worry, there was plenty of sausage to be cut. A hand signal from the other end indicated the bayonet would be no longer needed after five minutes more and back it came.

I knew no more until a little later when I got up and casually walked back to the New Zealanders. It is hardly correct to say walked back when we were packed in so tightly you had to step over bodies all over the place. I observed a hole big enough for a man to pass through and step onto the main through assembly. I was told they were waiting for the train to stop, then the two Newsies were going to go at dusk, if possible. And they did.

There was something about the outdoor life these Newsies led that adapted them quickly to bold action! I heard later they were gone about four days, which was pretty good. There was no way to get home, after all, but hundreds of Germans would be tied up looking for them.

The third and fourth days on the train were getting pretty rough for us with sanitation a major problem. The boys were getting sick all over the boxcar now and, of course, this brought on diarrhoea. When they changed guards at night, we hoped they would do something for us, but the doors only opened for five minutes under guard and no one was allowed out.

- CHAPTER 16 -

Stalag Luft I at Barth

We knew now we were going to Barth in the north of Germany and the guard had confirmed that it was getting close. A few hours later, the train pulled in and, once again, we were ditched on the outskirts of town in a field of green grass. It was like heaven, but we still lacked water to wash up. We were sheep counted in two's and our identity was checked. We then got on a lorry under guard.

They already knew that two of our boys were missing, because we had told them, a precaution we took to prevent their being shot as spies if they were picked up. We had not told them which two, and they didn't believe us until after the count. They then got mad all over again. "Hasn't the Fatherland been generous to you?"

The interpreter, one of the guards, told us to get off the lorry and line up in pairs for our first look at our new home. In front of us were the usual high, double-barbed wire fences with rolls of barbed wire in between and a warning wire on short posts inside that.

We stopped at the German Administration Offices right across from the main gate. Everybody was looking for lost buddies on the inside when I spotted Cameron. "What kept you?" he asked. That was a helluva long speech from someone I hadn't seen for six months and had thought could very well be dead! We had to go through the showers yet before they let us loose in the compound and I didn't argue about that, since we were pretty dirty. The shower was fine, but then it was back on with the soiled clothing. Then they hit us with louse powder and marched us back to the main gate. The soap was in my pocket — I was learning.

Once inside, Cam was waiting to pick me up and fill me in on what I would need. I was starved, and grateful for the crust of black bread he got me to hold me over. His hut, as it was called, was at the "old end" of the exercise field. My hut, just completed to meet the expanding need, was in a new compound with two other huts at the other end of the exercise field. Each room in my hut held several bunks; all two deckers. The gates between the compounds were always open except during searches and after dark.

Out in the centre compound, or sports field, the Germans had dumped some bales of straw and a stack of jute sacks. We filled a straw "tick" and, voila, we had a mattress. Then we looked for a bunk with at least five bedboards, and voila, we had our own pit. For a mug to drink from, we went to the dump and searched until we found a likely tin can with no rust on it. Then we used another tin can to make a handle. Cam got hold of a tool of sorts to cut the rims off the second can and cut three strips from the top to the bottom, one for the handle and two as bands to hold the handle in place. It was a real work of art. Then, all that was left was to boil it for sanitation! I often remember those makeshift tin mugs today, when I can make myself a nice cup of Nescafe and drink it in comfort.

At Barth we had a cookhouse run by our own boys. Everybody wanted a job in the cookhouse, because nobody ever got enough to eat. We saved these jobs for the big men who would not have survived on German rations. One husky Canadian, Harry Hands, dropped fifty pounds in no time. For breakfast they cooked up ersatz coffee. At noon they repeated the coffee and cooked up cabbage soup — if there was any cabbage given to us. Once a week, there was boiled barley and that was good because it was filling. There were also two potatoes and three slices of bread daily plus a piece of margarine and a spoonful of sugar. Without Red Cross parcels, many of us would have died from starvation.

I still had to make myself a plate, so I looked around at the old timers and found that they made up pans similar to a cake pan by joining three flattened out tin cans, again with the rims off. These were overlapped and set with a row of taps using a nail to dent them together. You ended up with a large, flat sheet. Then the sides were bent up and the corners folded over. I was the most surprised one of all when the one I made didn't leak. Cooking grease would have made it even better.

We were locked up tight at dusk and didn't get out till morning "appel," or roll count. The call for "everybody out" was a sight to behold, and an education to hear. The men arrived in all stages of undress, like a bunch of ragged urchins, and formed up in blocks of fifty men, five deep and ten across. How long the next stage took depended on the mood they were in.

The Officer-on-Parade was usually the Kommandant, or Commanding Officer, of the camp. He did not address us directly, but followed the usual system through his own "Non-Coms," which was when things often got out of hand. He assigned one poor German soldier to count each fifty men. Their thinking processes were not very agile and, as a matter of pride, the boys would mess up the count just by moving sideways or bobbing up and down. Somehow or other, Gerry could not pick this up and carry on. They had to start all over again each time, accompanied by the jeers of hundreds of P.O.W.'s who were all watching this in their large semi-circle with wide grins on their faces.

The Kommandant would then address our Senior British Officer, Warrant Officer First Class Dixie Deans, and tell him that was enough. Deans would immediately command us to straighten up and the count was then completed in nothing flat. Just who was the boss here, anyway? I first met Dixie Deans, at his request, as Camp Leader. Cam took me along to meet him the same way he met all new "Kriegies." He had an interest in how the war was going and some men he was trying to trace for their parents. There was no problem with my identity since I had been recognised by several people, but that was a major part of the job he was doing right in the camp. Every man must have a "sponsor," otherwise he was a suspect until identified. Security was vitally important to the safety of all of us.

After appel, we were on our own, and a crew from each hut went to the kitchen to collect our rations. When they returned, the food was divided up by an appointed person; to put it bluntly, someone we all trusted. Your share depended on the number of people in your "combine." Combining groceries to make up meals was very practical, especially with Red Cross parcels. Otherwise, each Kreigie would have had to open a can of meat large enough for three days and leave it open until he used it up. This was dangerous from a food poisoning standpoint.

Jack Cameron suggested he move to the new compound, where I was, and we could form a combine of two. He found a bunk next to mine so that our worldly possessions could be stowed nearby. We originally planned to take turns cooking, but I was so lousy at it that Cam took over that job and I did the dishes which, for lack of soap, we washed in sand.

Cam was more content with his new arrangement. It was easy to tell because the better he felt the more he bitched. He had been in a combine with five Welshmen and it had been hard to get a word in edgewise since they had a nasty habit of switching to Welsh.

Today you will get your first lesson in engineering — specifically, mechanical engineering. We are going to build a blower. Don't bother looking in the dictionary, you won't find it! Blowers are little cooking stoves capable of burning nearly anything, dry or damp. Blowers were used for centuries by the natives of Bongo Bongo and adapted readily to use in German prisoner of war camps where residents were half bongo anyway. First you take a bedboard, preferably someone else's, and cut it in half before you get caught. You then have a base board for two blowers. This is a good idea because the first one will end up in the ditch if it doesn't work. From here on it gets complicated. You make a fan at one end and a small open furnace pot at the other with a wind tunnel in between. Now you crank up the fan and blow air under the pot. If air comes up under the pot, you've got a blower.

Fuel for hut heating was strictly rationed to one briquette per day, per man. A steady wood supply for cooking was never available and so a blower became a prisoner's most valuable

125

possession. It would burn nearly anything from wet leaves to old newspapers, cardboard, shavings and even legs off chairs, using very little fuel of any sort. Before the war became more mobile, our supply lines for Red Cross parcels had been good but, by the time I entered the camp, we had been cut back to one parcel for each two men. That's when combines paid off, because we pooled everything anyway.

None of the huts was provided with running water. The only source was the kitchen and the washroom, both a hundred yards from our billet. Cam and I brought a two gallon bucket of water over each day to wash ourselves or our clothes, but these buckets were shared with others in our room. We then heated water over the blower and had a cup of tea or brew.

Doing laundry was called doing Dhobe, an East Indian word meaning your shirt is dirty. Although real soap was scarce, that Snap hand cleaner the Germans called soap was sometimes available because everyone hated to use it. Cam was an artist with this stuff. He got a broom handle somewhere and attached a can to the end so that it looked like a tin plumber's plunger and threw in the soap, hot water and dirty shirt. He was relentless. Two hours later, his Dhobe stick was still bashing away. I'll concede his shirts were whiter than mine but, boy, were they ever thin.

I have not yet mentioned the "circuit," the social hub of the P.O.W. camp. The circuit was a well-worn path in the playing field compound, or centre compound. It circled the football field just inside the warning wire. All important conversations would start on the circuit, as it was the only place with total verbal privacy. Escape plans or upcoming divorces were all grist for the circuit mill. Some nice summer evenings, there were hundreds of Kriegies on the circuit going round and round, or sitting a little farther in to watch the soccer game in progress. Above all, the circuit was where rumours started and, in the world of the hopeful, this made up a big part of our daily life. After all, Turkey was coming into the war wasn't she? This rumour started up every Friday morning for some reason or other and continued to pop up until the very end of the war!

The circuit was where we digested our most private news from back home. The mail, via the International Red Cross, was intermittent and sometimes non-existent, so it was not unusual to wait six months for a reply to a letter. In fact, some of our best laughs were a result of this. One of our boys sent a letter asking for socks. That letter took three months to get home. His mother wrote him back immediately asking what colour of socks. That letter from her took three months. So far six months had elapsed and still no socks. At this rate, it would take one year to get socks. That lady wasn't stupid, but in a way it was our own fault because in our own letters we told them as little as possible, so that they wouldn't worry. On top of that, the German censors cut lots of holes in our messages!

The ultimate extension of the above story happened to a boy from Winnipeg. His name was Schofield and he was a natural when it came to telling a story. First though, let me point out that, as P.O.W.'s, our pay was sent home each month. After a year as a prisoner, Schofield wrote his mother and asked for his bank balance. He knew it would take a total of six months to find out, and was content spending his waiting time dreaming about what he could do with his money after the war. His mother must have been very impressed with the way his total was building up so she wrote back, "GUESS." Schoffield, showing admirable restraint, wrote back and made his guess. When the reply came back this time, a full year and a half had passed, and her reply was "WRONG, GUESS AGAIN."

The circuit also supplied the essential disposal surface for sand dug out of tunnels. When freshly dug, it was moist and dark and hard to hide, but the Kriegies could dump it on the circuit a little at a time and scuff it in. There were two tunnels going on at that time — one from the hut next to ours and the other from the wash-house. I will bet every P.O.W. camp in Germany had an on-going escape plan, for that matter. Every now and then, the Germans would leave a posten box unmanned in error. Then the guys scrambled! Sometimes three or four would manage to get over the wire to run and hide. Sometimes they would be gone for four or five days. It took guts! That had just happened at our camp, and three got away.

Cam's mail was arriving now. He was shot down six months ahead of me, but had spent months in a German hospital. Part of his foot had been amputated, and he would have a permanent limp unless a special shoe could be moulded. He told me his family had been in touch with mine. I was grateful for that, especially since my own mail was not yet arriving. It was during this period that Cam had the unpleasant task of telling me that Evelyn, my only sister, had died. While nursing at Sick Children's Hospital, she had contacted tuberculosis at the age of twenty-two from a patient while on a short transfer to the sanatorium at Islington. She had passed away at the same time I was reported missing-in-action. Although Evelyn and I had been close friends all our lives, it was my parents I worried about. They must have thought their whole family was wiped out.

The men who had gone over the fence had not yet been missed and it was time to tell the Germans. Once again, they didn't believe us and did nothing. The next morning at wake-up parade, the Germans were confronted by a strange sight; instead of ten men in the front row, there were nine men and an empty pair of boots. So far this was just one of those foolish British Kreigie games, or so they thought, but they left us standing while they went through the barracks to count everybody and found no one. Then the panic was on! They moved all of us, at that time about nine hundred men, into a centre compound (the one with the football field) and did a sheep count by funnelling us through two at a time. Once through the funnel we were free to wander, so some of us casually wandered out to the warning wire and, a few minutes later, went half-way around the circuit until we were behind the others waiting to go through the funnel. We then joined the crowd, without being noticed, and went through again.

Hours later, the guards advised the Commanding Officer that the count was complete, and presented him with the figures. It would seem they were holding sixty-five too many prisoners!

The Kommandant, who by now was furious, told the guards they would be there all night until they were correct in their count and ordered the identification files to be brought out. Each man was to be identified by his photo. Our own old timers had been through this before and brought their tea, mugs, blower and fuel supply with them. Cam told me to bring my beautiful new blower and he would bring the rest. Those "dog biscuits" and jam sure

128

tasted good and, believe it or not, the blower worked and a brew was boiled up in nothing flat. The top flap of a cardboard box supplied the fuel — Cam had made dire threats if it didn't!

One of our Kriegies was nearly blind and used a companion and a cane. When they led him through the funnel his cane, with the help of the companion, he accidentally hooked the photo file and it tipped onto the ground and got badly mixed up. This made us poor, nameless souls in a foreign country, but that isn't what the Gerrys called us! My, oh my! Things were out of hand by now, and the guards were terrified they would be sent to the Russian Front. Dixie Deans stopped us and told us that was enough. He asked to speak to the Kommandant and told him that, in exchange for future favours, he would arrange an easy and fast count now. Only the names of the three missing P.O.W's would be supplied. We lined up for Dixie and gave the Germans an accurate count in ten minutes flat, and were dismissed. A ten minute count had taken all day!

Soccer was the big sport for us and over half the boys were on one team or another. We had several professional players from the British Isles and several School Boy Internationals. We had representation from each of the four levels of pros. Most Canucks were high on the list of athletics, but not in soccer. I discovered there was a lot more finesse in soccer than meets the eye. Andy Rogers and Rodger Rousseau both excelled at the sport. Most of us would watch these games for hours. When big name games were being played, even the German officers came over. No one had to tell them the game was on, they heard it through their own grape-vine.

Paddy Kerr was a long time Kriegie, and a long time German watcher. He knew every building the guards came out from and where they probably were going when they did come out. He knew with stop watch precision what time the guards were changed. He often had a name for each guard. Paddy Kerr, fearless and dedicated, had gone over the wire successfully more often than any other R.A.F. prisoner. In the Fall of 1943, he tried again, using our hut as a base. The only prop he needed for this performance was a chair. He had the warning wire, just a few feet high, plus two rows of barbed wire to cross. The two barbed wire rows were six feet across with loose rolls of wire in between; overall, about eight feet high. He waited until dark and, if successful, his plan would place him in the Germans' own barrack compound unguarded.

He asked one of the boys to place the chair where he could use it as a stepping stone, then no one went near that chair for two hours, allowing the guard to become used to seeing it. The ground supports for the posten box were only ten feet away and, on the guard's other side, a spirited game of ring toss over the net was in progress. Paddy took up position sitting on a rather high window sill with his feet dangling outside. The sun was beginning to move down now and, from where Cam and I stood, the whole panorama was visible, including the guard and his mounted machine-gun. In a split second, Paddy smoothly put down his book and dropped to the ground. He moved quickly to the chair, stepped on it with his left foot, made a long step to the warning wire post with his right foot, and jumped up. He caught the top wire and swung over the first wire and then the second wire. He was over! He dropped to the ground before the guard had even realized what was going on. Paddy then ran behind a building, out of the line of fire. The guard panicked and it took him a full minute to blow his whistle. Without a target, he was completely frustrated. Then out came the whole German Army!

Unfortunately, Paddy had sprained his ankle when he dropped to the ground and had to surrender. Oh well, a few more weeks in the "digger" didn't bother Paddy Kerr. It gave him time to plan his next escape!

Inside our billets, sanitation was our own responsibility but, outside the hut, it was done by Russians who, to all intents and purposes, were slaves. These were not soldiers, they were civilians who had not yet been drafted into the Russian Army. Their story, although not translated to me specifically, was always similar. Eleven thousand of these captured civilians were marched, on foot, from Russia, a distance of at least a thousand kilometres, during the brutal winter weather. More than half of them froze to death or starved. Then when they arrived at Barth, they were put under cold showers and died of exposure by the hundreds. Evidently there were only five hundred left at the time of our arrival and they were still dying. They were tattered, filthy and utterly without education. In the German officers' quarters, they drank from the toilet bowls, but we understood that they had never seen such a thing before. They were starving to death, and they even went through our pitiful garbage daily.

Their duties included emptying the sanitation pots for all eight hundred of us. They mended the fences, dug the post holes and they did this on smaller rations than we received and lost weight on. They operated the horse-driven carts to the dumps and kept their mouths shut when our boys were hiding underneath. They quickly learned to be middle-men for the Germans and the prisoners, and they did enough bartering on their own to survive, even if it was risky.

I learned pretty quickly, myself, to barter over the fence with a German guard looking on, but not letting on. He would get more than his share from the Russians, and I use the plural because it was safer to implicate two than one. Our medium was cigarettes and the demand was constant. I took what I could get and fired my cigarette pack over the fence at the Russian. One day it might be a cabbage and another day a turnip, but bread was what we wanted most. If mail was getting through and cigarettes more plentiful, the price would jump. Dixie Deans stepped in once and notified us there was to be no trading that day. It took three days and prices dropped five hundred per cent and a big, one kilo loaf was back down to two packages of Canadian cigarettes. This was a brown loaf with a thin crust and it was like cake to us. Our own regular bread was black — actually dark, dirty grey — and had spots of green mould on the outside and contained fifteen per cent sawdust. They were able to store this bread over the winter by burying it in bunkers of sawdust.

"Dear Elmer, I have a Grandmother in Germany. Have you met her?"

Any letter from home was welcomed and became public property.

"I am glad you were shot down before flying became dangerous!"

"You have become a Daddy," in a letter mailed ten months after he left home.

"But don't worry, my friend is going to send you cigarettes."
Nice touch!

I had received no mail yet from Canada, but a few letters had reached me from Scotland and England. Aunt Jeannie advised me that she had heard from Mother about Evelyn. Jeannie's own family were all well. Jim, Mom's brother in London, wrote telling me to keep my pecker up. It was through contact with new arrivals in our P.O.W. camp, though, that a sense of the reality of the war going on outside these fences returned. It was now late summer of 1943. The new boys told me the bombing was much more accurate than it had been earlier. Target marking had really improved but, unfortunately, losses were still very high in Aircrews. Mass production gave us many more planes, but the supply of new crews was always critical. It took a long time to train a crew and the crews then were averaging only six operations before they were shot down! These heavy losses had been going on for two years now.

There were many things going on inside our camp that the Germans did not know about. We had an excellent security system which went into action the minute a German or a stranger entered a compound. Every hut had a security team, but even many of our own did not know it existed. We had a radio and received daily news from Britain. We also had German news, which we divided by two. We had people who could make look-alike German uniforms and writers and printers for work papers and passes. We also had candle makers and electricians to cross up or rewire circuits and tunnellers whose ambition was to build, or dig, the longest tunnel in Germany. And, they were busy!

Our daily newsreader appeared in our hut each evening at dusk. We posted a guard at the door and gathered around to hear the day's news from Britain. Our spirits went up and down like a back house lid, depending on this report. The Allies, at last, had the Nazis on the run in North Africa. This was probably the first major good news story of the war since the Battle of Britain and we responded like school children! In response, the German newspaper stated that "Our elastic defences have drawn back to reinforce tomorrow's offensive." We loved it!

Basketball was a tremendously popular sport in Barth, and

we had several leagues going at any one time. A game that always drew a crowd was the Canadians vs. the Poles and Czechs. The "Canadian" name covered Americans as well if they were wearing R.C.A.F. insignia. My height left me about two feet short of being a super star, so they made me a referee for the second league, but it was exhausting work. Those guys would rather argue than shoot. It was good fun though — the arguments I mean.

After the disastrous defeats of the German Army in North Africa, the Italians, who were working as guards at Barth, were in a precarious position, since the Italian Army had put out peace feelers to the Allies. The only terms acceptable to the Allies would be total surrender, and after the loss of half a million men captured, killed or injured in North Africa, the Italians had lost their will to fight and did indeed surrender. Hitler was furious and forced many to work for the Nazis. His flank was exposed in Italy itself and Germany did a hasty retreat from North Africa into Italy to strengthen all their other positions. The guards at Barth who had been looking in, were now looking out. We had new neighbours! Germans were again in the posten boxes and the price of cabbage went up.

One of my favourite people now pulled off one of the funniest and most effective escapes any of us had ever seen. I had been tipped off about the event and just happened to be sitting outside when it happened. Short, stocky, and a master boxer, Burglar Bill was from Glasgow and proud of it. He was fearless, and even looked like mischief. It was broad daylight, and Bill was wearing a matted jacket like the Russian workers wore and an old European-style cap. In his hand, he had a hammer made of wood and a dummy pair of pliers. He walked over to the corner posten box and waved at the guard with his tools indicating he would have to climb up. The guard nodded. Bill then walked away and came back with a six-rung ladder, again waved at the guard, and stepped over the warning wire. At the top, he fooled around with the wire a minute then used the ladder laid on top to go to the far side of the double, eight foot fence. He intentionally dropped his hammer outside, called to the guard and pointed to his hammer and, without waiting for a reply, he dropped to the ground from the ladder. He picked up his hammer and ladder and moved back about ten yards and sat on the ground for a rest. When the guard got tired of watching him, Bill got up and walked away — far away. He was gone for two to three days, but came back quite content. A little digger time didn't bother him. He was drinking beer when they caught him.

Our main tunnel was doing rather well and I, myself, had been down to help, when something unforeseen happened. The horse-drawn honey cart had to detour and crossed over the tunnel. The cart carried a full load and the sheer weight was too much on those narrow wheels. The cart sunk up to its axles. Our boys sent out urgent signals in case anyone was trapped below. Regardless of the horrible perfume, dozens of P.O.W.'s tried to move the cart before the Gerrys caught on, but the Kommandant knew right away and the jig was up.

The Gerrys then brought in heavy equipment and ran it back and forth to trace the tunnel's origin in the washroom and soon had it figured out. There went three month's work and dreams, but we didn't give up. "Let's try again while we are still young!" "Tomorrow be alright?"

Our "cooler" or "digger" was doing a thriving business these days. This "jail within a jail" was filling up fast with tunnellers and escapers, plus a few "insolent" P.O.W.'s who told guards what to do with their rifles.

It was late fall now and we knew winter would be right behind it. We were in the north of Germany where the weather got quite severe. Due to a poor assortment of clothing and no assistance from the Germans, we would be spending a good part of our winter indoors.

Shaving and washing in the mornings was usually a matter of heating water on a blower and using a home-made pan to hold the shaving water. The only alternative was a tap of cold water in the lavatory — but don't confuse this with a washroom. We had a forty-seater cut out of long planks and don't think that wasn't drafty in the winter.

I am due on the basketball court soon but, in the meantime, there's a top game coming up that I want to see. Peaches Bundy, Ab Rey and a few other Toronto boys will be playing. Some of my buddies are already "sitting in the front row," which means their respective butts are on the ground. Al Hayworth, Pop Kingdon, Bill Charlesworth, Freddie Churchyard, Ted Woolley, McQuarrie, Zeke Fox — you name 'em, we got 'em. Half the camp will turn out for this game and what cigarettes are left will be on the line. These games were played on sand so there was no dribbling. That's enough to make you go to the bathroom, isn't it?

Since we were locked in at night, a three-seater was provided at the end of the centre hall. The Russian workers emptied this from the outside every morning. Under the centre containers was a trap door leading to a well advanced escape tunnel. Once more, we were under attack for bedboards for tunnel shoring! This tunnel was perilously close to the front fence at Barth and would be in immediate danger of discovery if anything suspicious happened.

I once had a close one while I was carrying a bucket of sand down the centre hall. The front door opened and in walked a guard. There was no one else in the hall, and I walked past him as casually as I could. To this day I don't know why he didn't ask where the sand came from! I turned into our room and immediately started scouring pots — any pots. Heaven knows I had enough sand to scour a hundred pots.

The boys checked to see where the guard had gone, then resumed packing socks with sand. These socks had open toes and a release string. When you pulled the string, out dribbled the sand. Two socks, one down each leg, were held together by a string across the shoulders. Very effective! Anyone going on the circuit took one set along. Tons of sand was moved this way and got to the circuit unseen.

Down the road some mornings, we would hear and sometimes see the German soldiers marching along singing four-part harmony (that is my description only since I'm not too well versed on the subject). It was enjoyable to listen to as I missed music as part of everyday life. Their marching alone was musical since they wore heavy hob-nailed boots and drilled as ordered. The Master Race was showing off in front of us. We hesitated to tell them it was distracting our tunnellers!

On a day when a good batch of mail arrived, I got two letters. One from Dad, about fifty-five years old at that time and carrying on still at work. Reading between the lines, he was ready for retirement. He never seemed to have recovered from Evelyn's death. Mother was all right. I had written requesting a Gillette safety razor and blades be sent in my personal parcel. She had the Dickens of a time to find one and, finally, went to the Air Force Base at The Hunt Club where they got one for her. All this amazed me when I heard about it. It was the first time I realized there were wartime shortages in Canada.

The second letter was from Mary Slatter, my boyhood friend, John's, sister. Bless her! You can't imagine how important letters were to us.

I still hadn't received my first personal parcel yet, a parcel permitted to be ten pounds in weight, twice a year, no food allowed.

- CHAPTER 17 -

Stalag Luft I to Hydekrug via Cattlecar

A Bulletin appeared on the board bearing Dixie Deans' signature informing us we would all be moving in three days time. We would be moved in the usual cattle cars to Hydekrug near Koenigsburg. North and east, in other words; no place for a winter vacation.

A decision by the escape committee was made to close down the tunnel under our hut and secure it as well as possible for future use. It still had about twenty yards to go, I believe.

Packing for a move was a major job, since you could only take what you could carry. First priority was pots, pans, mug, spoons, and knives. Clothing came next, along with your blanket, although once you were dressed there wasn't much more clothing to worry about. Your blanket made a good dunnage bag to carry other items. Food was next, then cigarettes and, finally, your blower, soap if any, a towel and squares of newspaper if you were so lucky. One other thing — if you can carry it, steal a bedboard, break it in two, and carry it for use in the blower. You could boil almost ten pots of water on one bedboard!

Managing that load really depended on whether we walked or got transported to the cattle cars.

Once packed, we sat back hoping that, when we left, the Germans would give us one of our own food parcels with our bread ration or, even better, when we arrived at the train in case we had to carry it.

I had been at Barth for many months and had a pretty good idea now of prisoner of war routines and problems, but food and health would always be on top of the list.

> "Dear Son,
> I sent you a birthday cake all covered in your favourite creamy topping but the Red Cross sent it back."

That one was posted on the bulletin board. And,

> "Yes Dear. Try Hard Tack biscuits next time. They are the only thing that will survive three month's delivery!"

The Gerries apparently couldn't read. The boxcar distinctly said forty men and there we were again with sixty. When we got in, Cam and I moved well back in the car and lay down to establish our space. It was always debatable if everybody could lie down at one time. As we had hoped, we did get an American Red Cross Parcel, and we had been trucked to the siding. German travel rations included one-third of a loaf of black bread, margarine and a four inch long piece of horsemeat sausage, approximately one-and-one-half inches in diameter.

All the other members of my crew who were N.C.O.'s were making this move with us, but were in a different boxcar. Willis and George Mott had found a bunch of Scots to chum with. MacFarlane had a back problem, but was on his feet O.K. and had dropped over to say hello last week. He had heard from his family and all was well. None of us had had any real news.

We had done all this before, but you never got used to it. I think the lack of direct sunlight had something to do with it. There were two small windows in the cattle cars, but they were too high up to see from. Even when it was cool outside, it was steamy inside. When we slowed down, the boys prayed it was for a pit stop. The buckets were just about full and, once again, the heat, the crowding, the lack of sanitation, and the lack of medication left us all ripe for another session of diarrhea followed by dysentery.

The Kriegies started to yell for a stop, but received no word from outside the boxcar. The two guards assigned to the inside were getting nervous. It was obvious they didn't trust what we might do. When the train stopped, one of the guards held his weapon on us in an attempt to move us to one end of the car. The other guard stood by the door waiting until it was opened from the outside to reveal that we were two hundred yards from the station. Several of the men who just couldn't wait any longer brushed the guard aside and marched toward the field, and the others, fearing the worst, surrounded the guards so that they couldn't take aim. Two other boys grabbed the bucket from the boxcar and ditched the contents three feet from the doors. Five minutes was all it took to get them all back on the train. All this time, the boys were talking to the guards telling them not to panic, and that these young men were all Christians and preferred to give rather than to receive. So far they had certainly proven that!

We were all relieved, which was the original intent, and prayed that the train would move out from this troubled spot before a lot of people ended up in a Gestapo prison. Now the boys on the floor were singing, "Oh, what a relief it is." At 2:00 a.m., the train pulled out and oh, what a relief that was!

We slept better than expected that night. Those floors sure were hard, though.

On the third day, Jack and I opened our Red Cross food parcel. This one was from the United States and contained an assortment of foods altogether different than the Canadian or British parcels. More instant coffee, less powdered milk, less butter, more jam and, of course, the brands differed. There were Camels and Chesterfields rather than Players and Sweet Caps. This was my first American Red Cross parcel, but it was not new to Cam, who was shot down six months earlier, and don't think I didn't razz him on this! "Say, I wouldn't mind that chocolate bar for breakfast right now."

The stress and discomfort resumed, as once again there were no pit stops. These people were not human.

We couldn't use our blowers in the boxcars very easily because the smoke would have choked us. So, our spuds were just stored and our oatmeal couldn't be boiled. We resorted to black bread, margarine, cheese and jam. By noon, the rumour mill had spread the information that we would arrive at our destination later that same day. By the time we pulled in, our captors determined that it was too late to unload us, so we were left locked up until morning. We were grateful that, before we left, we had thought to half fill a cooking pot with fresh water and, although the water wasn't fresh, our forethought did pay dividends now that the big bucket of drinking water was all gone.

When we were unloaded, we gasped big gulps of fresh air. It sure felt good. Even the two guards had a smile after that long ride was over. The Gerries marched us to the camp, but allowed us a wagon for all the opened Red Cross boxes.

When we arrived, we were surprised at how large a camp Hydekrug was. We were all going into one "lager" where hundreds of men were already settled in. Then there was another entirely separate lager with nearly one thousand R.A.F., non-commissioned officers.

- CHAPTER 18 -

Hydekrug Luft 6

For all intents and purposes, ours was a Canadian lager. The Gerries liked to do that — separate us, then try to play one Ally against the other. We were assigned to a hut and ditched our baggage. Cam immediately went on the scrounge while I walked over to get our food parcel from the wagon. Cam made sure all our bedboards were present, plus an extra one. Then I went to the straw pile to fill two pillowcases. This took a half hour; they are hard to fill.

Next came the water taps for a wash up, and a pan of water to make tea. Tea and a cigarette, what could be better than that! For a virile twenty-two year old Canadian lad to admit that, things must have been tough!

Once again, kindling-sized wood was going to be hard to find, so Cam had already popped the extra bedboard and cut it into sticks. That ensured we were O.K. for a few days. We were at the back of our room near the stove. I had the upper bunk and, in those days, I could make it.

Dixie Deans was in such high esteem that he was chosen by acclamation as camp leader again, a position that included both lagers. The other lager was designated as "A" and ours as "K."

The soccer leagues were organized within a few days of arrival and were soon in full swing. There was a senior league game at least twice a week, and there was the equivalent to two

141

full British soccer teams in the camp. This was terrific football to watch, but knowing all the players made it that much better.

Basketball was of a pretty good calibre, too. There was one outstanding player. Although his name is long gone from my memory, his shots on the hoop live on. He was an American in the R.C.A.F. and a terrific showman, but quite unassuming. During practice one day, he showed us a couple of tricks in ball control. His arms were very long and he would spin the ball on one finger while standing inside the court and yet, was controlling the ball two feet away for a long time. He then took the ball to the opposite foul line, turned, and shot in one motion and sunk the ball without touching the backboard. Everybody cheered and laughed. One of our boys said, "I'll bet you can't do that again". He did! No one could touch him without getting a foul!

The theatre group was active, with big plans for the winter season. A play was already on the books, and auditions for actors were being held.

The escape committee was meeting again, but there was no word of a plan yet. If anyone approached them with a particularly bright idea, all tunnelling stopped temporarily, and that man was given every assistance. Passport, travel passes, money, a suit, food to travel and, if possible, an outside contact. The suit would be converted from a uniform and dyed. Passports and travel passes were forged.

At the end of August, 1944, I developed acute appendicitis. There were no facilities to handle this at Hydekrug. The British Army Major, who was our one and only doctor, had no instruments to speak of except a scalpel and scissors, no drugs nor anaesthetics. He talked to the German Commanding Officer who agreed, if I would give my parole and not try to escape, to take me into the hospital in Koenigsburg, about twenty-five kilometres away. When I arrived, I was pretty darn sick, but they handcuffed me to the bed frame anyway. Two French doctors inspected me and they decided to operate although there was a language problem between us.

The doctors told me to get undressed and pointed down the hall. After the guards unlocked me, I never saw them again. I took off what little clothing I had on and dragged myself down

142

the hall in my birthday suit. Spotting a door to one side, I opened it and walked in. There were three or four nurses smoking and talking, who immediately broke into great bursts of laughter at the sight of me and started to clap and cheer. I was helpless, since I didn't speak German, but I gave them a phonetic interpretation of nichts vorstechen (I don't understand). One nurse then took me by the hand and led me to the operating room orderly. Five hours later, I found myself back in the ward room cot, but without the handcuffs. My head was fuzzy, but otherwise I felt all right. A nurse and an orderly sat me up, then stood me up and walked with me for five minutes. I then went to sleep until morning when they awakened me and got me dressed.

When they were out of the room, two other men came in and tried to carry on a conversation with me, but there was too much of a language barrier. I didn't know their nationality, but I assumed they were prisoners of the Germans. They gave me a written note which I promptly hid in the worn sole of my shoe. They disappeared fast — real cloak and dagger-like — and in came two German soldiers to escort me back to Hydekrug by car. On my return, they put me in the "recovery ward," which I hoped had some truth to its name.

The doctor lived in the recovery ward with his own room at one end, but he had no other special privileges. He was a long-term prisoner from the failed Dunkirk landing in 1940, who had volunteered to stay on the beaches and help the thousands of wounded before he was taken prisoner.

The orderlies in this hut were volunteer Aircrew men who deserved a great deal of credit for the health care work at Hydekrug. Most of the patients were chronic bed-care patients. Exceptions would be a diabetic with no insulin available, a mental case who was a twenty-three year old boy who kept seeing flak coming up at him all day long, and recovery cases such as my own. There were about ten patients at all times. Now the doctor, who had been a prisoner too long, was a bit around the bend. This could have been a temporary condition, but his condition appeared to be very real. He had gotten hold of a "sweet potato." (For those whose education has been neglected, a sweet potato, if you stretch the point, was a musical instrument on which you could achieve a full scale of notes provided your lips didn't flop from trying. The notes were quite pure, but I refuse to elaborate on pure what.)

There was an on-going list of men requesting circumcision, which was quite a fad but very painful, since we had no drugs available. Our doctor allowed two in at a time. The pain was not at the time of the operation, but later whenever the weapon felt a need to expand. The orderlies got a fiendish delight out of hanging Marilyn Monroe's picture at the end of the poor guy's bed. The doctor remained quite distant from all this pain and suffering by playing his sweet potato all day and half the night. The other patients survived by venting their vective until exhausted, then falling asleep — really the only escape other than suicide with a dull knife.

Cam came over to advise me that we had received a Turkish parcel made up entirely of dried fruit, plus one box of gelatin candy gums. Cam felt that since I might be in there for quite some time, it might be best if he ate up the apricots, prunes, figs and raisins. I came back fast on that one and told him to keep his hands off my figs!

Another boy who was a patient here had lost interest in food. They felt he would starve to death if he wasn't taken care of. It was quite a sight to watch those orderlies trying to pamper him. One day, they arrived with a big smile. They had, somehow or other, gotten hold of an egg. This was for Brian. First, they asked him how he would like it cooked. He said he didn't care. Here was a boy with open sores all over his legs from malnutrition who turned down an egg, when one thousand men around him would have sold their shirt to get it. Finally, they soft boiled it, flipped the lid off, and got two small spoonfuls into him. Brian then turned his back on them. What a heartbreak!

A few days later I was able to walk out of there. Since I was on the inside of the wire already, there was no check in. Most of the boys were out on the circuit when I returned to my bunk, and it took me a minute or two to figure out what was different. It was the smell! After sniffing about for a while, I looked under the bunk below me and found the coal box for holding our daily ration of briquettes. The briquettes, however, were not in the box but stacked neatly beside it. Inside the box was a hard working mash. I could see the first lumps in it, especially the apricots and all those raisins.

There was no one around at the moment, so I laid down for a nap, figuring there must be a basketball game on. I hoped Cam and I didn't own one hundred per cent of this one or we would be tight for a month. Also, this was the first time I had ever slept in a brewery! Cam usually slept below me, but had moved to my bunk when I was away to keep his nose from getting pickled by the brew underneath.

The Red Cross had sent us a load of books, so we spent hours reading after we were locked in at dusk. At 9:00 p.m., our only three light bulbs went out until 8:00 a.m., and that's when all our skimping and saving paid off. A tin can full of German margarine with a cloth wick made it possible to read after dark. It was not smokeless, however, and it did attract the fleas we had inherited from the Russians.

I had taken the note from inside the hole in my shoe and delivered it to Dixie Deans with an explanation of where it came from. A verbal message came back from Dixie saying it was important, and he thanked me. No further comment was required.

It was a month before we got the next Red Cross parcel. The only extra from the Germans these days was a pot of boiled barley. We looked forward to it; at least it was filling. When the supply of parcels began to dry up, we added two more men to the combine, Zeke Fox from Truro, Nova Scotia, and Alex McQuarrie from Rainy River, Ontario. Alex was another bank boy about my own age. Zeke was a railway man about five foot four and all muscle. None of us was married.

Early one morning in July, 1944, the rumour mill started working overtime and this one was for true. A repatriation program had been worked out by the International Red Cross. An exchange would be made and some of our boys would go home. Those that were chosen would be men who had been permanently injured and could never return to combat. Howie Copeman, a buddy of ours who had flown Hampdens, fell into this category. Howie had been originally in a German P.O.W. Hospital at Schleswig-Holstein, then in Dulag Luft where he, Cam and Don

Morrison first met. Don would also be on the "repats" ship. Stu Murray, who would also be going, promised to contact my Mom and Dad when he hit Toronto. Both of them would probably be checked in to Christie Street Hospital for assessment. I was very happy, both for the Kreigies involved, and for my mother and father who would know I really was all right. The problem, of course, was that in our efforts to keep their minds at ease, we were telling them nothing!

After a heartbreaking delay or two in the negotiations, they finally lined up, or propped up, the repats and began moving them out. Every Kreigie in the camp was there to wave them off and wish them the best. They had all earned this the hard way. God bless them all.

We lost an R.A.F. boy shortly after through sheer stupidity on the part of a posten box guard. This Kriegie had walked over to the warning wire to dispose of a dish pan of wash-up water. When he sloshed the water, the guard shot him. Every available P.O.W. lined up on the circuit and walked past the guard to stare at him. We wanted identification for after liberation. I don't know if the guard was frightened, but the Kommondant was and yanked the guard. We heard the next day that he was on his way to the Eastern Front before the International Red Cross heard about it. Our request for a military march past was turned down.

We still received the news every day, and it was getting more and more up-beat. Our news readers appeared at dusk each day and read from a script, then moved on. Gerry was still in the dark as to how we received our news. They had never been able to find a radio.

Our Kriegies decided to lead the Gerries on just for laughs, but first, all valuable contrabands were removed from the room to be set up as a radio receiving centre.

One of our men walked over to a hut corner where there was a row of rooms, side by side like a condominium. He started to peek out and, then, pulled his head in fast. This was so obvious, they should have caught on right there. Instead, the guard waved to a "ferret," who was a roving guard like an internal policeman. The ferret went to the main gate very quietly and, sure enough, within minutes, out came twenty Gerries in full uniform with bayonets fixed rushing around the corner. In the meantime, our phony look-out had retreated to the "radio room" where a table had been set up with a blanket over it. On top of the table was a large cardboard box also covered by a blanket. On the box was printed: "SILENCE. PROGRAM IN PROGRESS. THE NEWS FOLLOWS."

Our old wind-up gramophone was playing quite loudly and about one hundred men were crowded around the box cheering. The guards rushed in, but they didn't know what to do. The long bayonets were more of a hindrance than help and, of course, our boys started stepping back until the table was quite visible.

One of the guards got brave and jabbed the box with his bayonet. That's all it took to knock it off the table and, needless to say, there was nothing underneath. The Gerry Sergeant arrived just then and read the situation pretty fast. He called off his men and told them to line up outside. All the boys were cheering and clapping. The sergeant called out, "You all think you are so smart." He then shook his head and marched out with a grin. It had been his second radio call that year.

The day the Allies landed, we all knew about it. The excitement was unbelievable, but none of us stopped to think what still had to be accomplished to establish this foothold. As the months slid by, we had to be content with the slow but steady progress our armies were making. Judging by the number of new prisoners arriving every week, the bombing raids were continuing at an even heavier rate than ever.

One of the Kriegies in our room had drawn a big map on a square of cardboard and hung it on the wall. He marked the advances daily. Town after town was being recaptured, but we were still hundreds of miles to the east.

Discussions with the new prisoners told quite a story. Although the P.O.W.'s were being sent to Dulag Luft, as usual, they were not being held there very long before they were shipped out to regular P.O.W. camps, like the one we were now in. The regular camps were being expanded and new ones being built.

The most important story, however, had to do with a new gunnery technique the Luftwaffe had developed. This new technique, called SCHRAGE MUSIK, involved fitting twin, upward firing cannons in the cockpit of ME110 fighters. "Upward firing" was the secret to their success. Before this, a single-seater fighter could only hit what the plane was aimed at. But with these guns permanently mounted on an upward angle, if they could sneak up under a bomber without being seen, it was all over! All the fighter pilot had to do was ape the manoeuvres of the bomber, then fire wherever he wanted. The crew on the bomber could not see below to spot him. A mid under turret would now be a necessity! And, for the very old gunners, this is the same ME110 plane that used to have a crew of two!

The new arrivals also told us that the "German Bombers over Britain" was a terror from the past. Rockets were the latest menace, but not the old V1 type that ran out of fuel, then dropped. The new V2 was a high flying, fully programmed vehicle that could hit a pre-arranged target with no pilot on board. How the British people stood up to this nerve-wracking business I'll never know!

We must have been close to a launching site, because evening after evening we watched the smoke trails curling upward in the sky. At first we did not understand, because we had heard that the V1's were only marginally successful, but the new rockets that our Kreigie arrivals told us about would fit in with these.

One morning, we looked out to see the grounds covered with strips of silver paper about six inches long by one-quarter inch wide, their shiny surfaces glittering in the sunlight. When we looked up, there were still thousands of these strips floating in the breeze.

Our new arrivals laughed when they saw it. They had spent a lot of time dumping "window" as it was called. When it hit the slip stream, it separated and floated over a big area. At first, it completely confused the German radar operators. Each piece of window showed up on their screen as an enemy aircraft. This saved hundreds of Aircrew lives because radar could not direct the night fighters. Unfortunately, they were able to develop counter-measures.

Nothing very funny happened in the camp these days. At least, not like the boys trying to walk the circuit with a belly full of their home brew. Not very successfully, I might add.

Progress was being made, and our Canadian Army and Parachutists were a big part of it. We were collectively so very proud of them.

- CHAPTER 19 -

To Camp 357 - Thorn, Poland

Well, they had done it again! According to Dixie, we were to be ready to leave in forty-eight hours. We were being sent east into Poland to an army P.O.W. camp at Thorn (Torn), north and west of Warsaw. This would be a long trip by boxcar with no assurance of a Red Cross parcel yet, although we knew there were thousands of them in storage nearby. Dixie would be fighting hard on our behalf for them. Our argument was legit; they belonged to us. The news of this move was depressing to most of the Kriegies, as we were being taken further away from our armies. There were maybe fifty Poles serving in the R.A.F. with us who found the move exciting but, at the same time, didn't trust what the Germans could do to them. Their only protection was the uniform they wore.

The day before we marched out of Hydekrug, we watched a huge formation of American bombers heading south and east from us. They were under attack, and we watched breathlessly as the Gerry fighters dived to break-up the formation. A stray bomber was promptly pounced on by a dozen fighters and eventually was set on fire. All of this was going on five miles over our heads. As we watched, two more bombers caught fire and parachutes began to appear. Several fighters were spinning downward, and one of their chutes opened. Another one didn't but, when the formation carried on, it made us all feel better. We

149

were a long way from England, and some of those poor guys would be landing within a mile or two of our camp. I wanted so much to talk to them and get their feelings about how the Allies were doing at that very moment.

The travel rations doled out to us suggested a three day trip, so we knew we had better count on four. Cam and I divided the load between us. Our combine had crept to seven in number and was no longer efficient, so we had decided to dissolve it. Sammy Somers, our latest member, was a twenty year old from Calgary who hadn't been overseas more than a few months when he was shot down. He had needed some time in combine to find his feet, but would be O.K. now. Bill Reid, from Toronto, also went on his own. We had tried to help Bill but, when he wouldn't bother to eat or look after himself, he developed running sores on his legs from malnutrition. Cam and I were having it tough enough just looking after ourselves, even with the odd extra cabbage. Alex McQuarrie and Zeke Fox teamed off, and Art Harrison joined up with an R.A.F. type.

We headed out the main gates, not really knowing what lay ahead. A cart was being pushed along carrying one parcel for every six men. These would be divided on the train with plenty of bartering going on.

The Gerries had one innovation waiting for us when we arrived at the siding. All the boxcars were marked "forty men or eight horses," but we were already used to this being ignored. In the past, they put sixty men in one car — but sixty men in two-thirds of this space was much worse. They had run barbed wire across the inside of the car to form three sections, one section to the left of the opposite doors and another to the right. The guards brought a bench on board, and now they could sit and watch us behind the barbed wire barrier on either side and still open the sliding doors for ventilation. There were thirty P.O.W.'s on either side. Sitting up was possible. Lying down was impossible.

The Red Cross parcel was Canadian this time, and that was good. Most of us agreed their parcels were better planned. When we drew lots, Cam and I got a can of Spam, a tin of Klim powdered milk, a tin of strawberry and apple jam and a twenty-five pack of Sweet Caps. We then bet our jam against a can of

150

butter and won. That gave us the luxury of having both jam and butter.

We were on our way fairly quickly and settled in the best we could. We learned that the Gerries were afraid of delays because the trains were often attacked by fighter planes. That wasn't a very pleasant thought for us or the civilian prisoners who were the train crews. By nightfall we were exhausted.

The next day, the guards were just as tired as we were, so two new guards took over. One of them, wishing he had one of our cigarettes, offered to cut a Kreigie's hair for a cigarette. This started a thriving industry. Only one Kreigie was allowed through the door in the fence at a time. We also wanted to empty the latrine bucket as we rode along, but the guards said no. All of a sudden, no one wanted their hair cut. The next day was the same until about two o'clock. The guards had a lot of smoke blowing in their direction that day, and finally said, "One cigarette each to dump the bucket instead of just one." After about twenty minutes in an unnecessary huddle which was all for show, the Kriegies agreed and carried up the stinking bucket. One guard unlocked the outer door, then the inner door. Both guards then aimed their rifles and one of ours opened the door outside and tipped the bucket while the other helped from the rear. The accompaniment was tremendous.

> "Sweet Violets, sweeter than all the roses
> Covered all over from head to toe
> Covered all over with shit ... "

Our brave men from the bucket brigade returned to their mundane existence of eating off the floor and the guards sat back and enjoyed their smoke. Life could be pleasant.

We arrived at the station at Thorn about 10:00 a.m. and soon found out we had a long walk ahead of us. There was no transport available. We carried what we could, but many a load was being dumped. Dysentery was back with us again and, this time, the bleeding was heavier than ever. So far on this trip I had been fortunate. These long walks didn't help Cam with his bad foot, though.

Thorn turned out to be a huge army camp made up of several compounds, most of which were now open. There were no Air

Force in ahead of us, and a large number of the former residents had been moved out. Half the soldiers here were Canadians from Dieppe: Toronto Scottish, Essex Scottish, Royal Regiment of Canada and some Winnipeg boys. They were still put in chains every night at dusk. The list above does not preclude other Regiments being represented here, but indicates the ones I ran into myself. These army prisoners were represented by a British Senior Officer; in other words, the highest ranking P.O.W. in that camp. In the R.A.F. prisoner of war camps, the man was elected, usually by acclamation, so that some friction arose right at the start. We wanted Dixie Deans as our camp leader and no one else. This came to a head when a couple of Sergeants were charged with insubordination and Dixie Deans stepped in. They went at it hot and heavy for a while. Since all Air Force men were in a separate compound, even if the gates were open, a compromise was made where Dixie would continue as British Air Force Man of Confidence and the Army Colonel would continue as Senior British Officer of the Army.

This was very important to us, since most Air Force, especially the "Colonials" hated British Army discipline. They were mostly free spirits responsible to each other, within their own crews only. It sounds irresponsible, but it wasn't. Our lives were on the line every night, and we flew when ordered, but crew discipline was our own problem and yet no problem. Once we left England on each operation, we were on our own.

Although Dixie was a Warrant Officer First Class, there were many men who outranked him the minute their own commissions were announced. But Dixie proved his right to leadership time and time again by his decisive action and our willingness to follow. He didn't bend to the Gerries; if anything, he led the Gerries.

The Gerries did not solve their problem by jailing or shooting us, because we were holding thousands of their men prisoners, too. The Red Cross would have heard about their actions within twenty-four hours so, if they got too rough with us, their own men might have suffered.

Ours was really an R.C.A.F. compound with a few other nationalities present. Even at that, many of the Canadians had been separated from us when we left Hydekrug. Half the boxcars were shunted off, and ended up on an island in the Baltic.

The grounds here were very spacious. A new compound had just been opened to hold American Flyers, separated from ours by barbed wire, but access was easy. The Yanks were offering their bomber jackets for one hundred cigarettes. Fortunately, I had the smokes, or could barter for them, because this was something I needed. The flying jackets we wore under our coveralls were not too warm and gave no protection to our kidneys. My own jacket had been falling apart, but I was now all set for the winter ahead.

The Yanks loved to play baseball and held a good game every evening. Cam and I enjoyed watching these games and got to know quite a few of the army boys, particularly the Essex Scottish, who were such a colourful lot. It was softball they played, because baseball mitts were at a premium, but it was a very good grade similar to the fastball they played at the Beaches in Toronto. The umpire, Charlie Surpliss, was a Sergeant with the Toronto Scottish who had been a few years ahead of me at Jarvis Collegiate. He had been a Toronto policeman before the war for about a year and then joined up.

At dusk, these soldiers were ordered into their barrack room where they lay down in a row to be chained together. It was hard to believe this was happening in the Second World War! The barrack hut was then locked up for the night.

Within five minutes, they were out of their chains and playing cards at the table. They did this by using a sardine can twister which never failed!

There were several barter shops here. Everything for sale had a cigarette equivalent. You know, one pair of shoes, ten cigs; a shirt, fifteen cigs; and so on. The commission on the sale, three cigs. Oh! And don't get caught cheating, Mr. Storekeeper! Those latrines are very deep. And don't try to hang onto the seat, they will walk on your hands.

Justice here was sure and efficient, but it had nothing to do with the Senior British Officer, or the Nazis for that matter. These boys appointed their own camp control officers.

I found this association with the army boys to be refreshing and talked to a lot of them. This was not a Non-Commissioned

Officers' Camp, so most of them were Privates, but all ranks other than officers were here. Discipline by rank prevailed, but seldom showed. That was the Canadian way all right, and it worked O.K. here.

To get from the American compound to the outside, you had to cross a big empty field to one side of the compound. The field was surrounded by the usual barbed wire fence and posten boxes. These American boys jumped the fence one evening and started to run for the far side. They were spotted, and one of them was hit by machine-gun fire. The other one dropped to the ground and stayed there. Four Germans arrived, one of them an officer. They ordered the uninjured one to get on his feet but he refused.

"You will shoot me if I stand up," he announced, and he stayed on the ground until a Senior American Officer showed up along with the German Camp Kommandant.

The officer told the boy, "You can get up now. They wouldn't dare shoot you. There would be a riot." This was said more for the benefit of the Kommandant than the men. They took him to the digger, but at least he was alive. Finally the wounded man was taken to the camp infirmary. I hoped that at least they had some sulfa.

On Sundays we had a real treat. There was a road which ran alongside the camp and, on Sundays, dozens of girls walked slowly by and waved to us on the sly. We wondered how come so many girls? Then we found out. These were Polish girls who were slaves to the Nazis. Their sole job was to entertain the German soldiers on leave from the Russian front.

And that reminds me to tell you. The guns we heard in the distance were not the Allies. They belonged to the Russians who, according to the B.B.C., were advancing steadily toward the eastern Polish border. It seemed that this would be the last year of the war! What a beautiful thought that was, even if open to some question.

I had a small project in mind — to build a smaller portable blower that would weigh maybe less than two pounds. It took me a few days to lay out a pattern using newspaper. Next, I went back to the dump to find suitable pieces of metal or tin cans. This turned out to be easier than I thought. Our last shipment of

Canadian Red Cross parcels each contained Klim Powdered Milk in tins which were longer than most. When the rims were cut off and flattened out, I had a good sized sheet of metal. I found three of them and, within two days, I had the fan completed. Cam must have been impressed. All of a sudden, he stopped groaning and began to show some interest other than in frying pans and Dhobe sticks. He even came up with a piece of bedboard. I wonder who fell through the bunk that night?

The tunnel and firebox were not too difficult. Then, I just packed the insides of the firebox with mud. Clay would have been best, but this was an all sandy soil area. Complete now, except for the gearing, I finally settled for a leather shoe lace from the dump.

Our new blower worked very well and weighed less than two pounds. In the past, they had been too heavy to carry, and we invariably ended up leaving them behind. This one we could use at the side of the road. We packed it away for use on our next move, which might not be too far off, judging by the sound of the guns.

Our news reader that night advised us that Antwerp was now undamaged and in the hands of the Allies, but that forty miles of the river bank approach was still held by the Nazis.

Burt Hoeck, a soldier we knew from the Royal Regiment, came over to say hello one day. We put on the blower and made a cup of tea and shot the bull. He told us that, when he got captured at Dieppe, they had to remove his trousers to patch him up. They cut them off, which had left him with no trousers. He was still able to walk, however, and the Gerries made him join the line up and march down the street while they took propaganda movies.

One night last week, the Gerries had unchained them all and marched them over to a big warehouse on the grounds. They then set up a projector and showed them propaganda films, one of which had Burt in the front row with no trousers on, or anything else, either. A great cheer went up from all his buddies. He couldn't even fight back!

Burt had a drug store in Trenton. If you see him, be sure to remind him. He'll hate you.

The American lager was filling up fast. It was easy to guess why. Our readers were telling us of the large number of aircraft that were being produced and available for operations. The Nazi fighter planes, although they were still very active, were not as numerous.

Inexperienced Allied Aircrew and fighter pilots were a problem now. We couldn't train them fast enough and were sending them on operations before they even knew where to look for trouble. Some of these boys were showing up in P.O.W. camps still shaking.

The figures may seem contradictory, but they were not. They simply meant that we were losing as many men but getting twice as many raids done. Men were obviously expendable! The Germans were probably also running low on aircrews.

We were too far east at Thorn to see our own bombers, but the rolling thunder of the big guns east of us was constant now. We wondered how long it would be before they moved us again and in what direction?

For the first time since coming to Thorn, we received a full Red Cross parcel for each man, as we were supposed to. It was like a birthday party. Cam was able to show off his culinary arts with potatoes fried in butter and Spam right out of the frying pan, then topping it off with rice pudding in a creamy sauce. Man oh man!

- CHAPTER 20 -

Exit from Thorn to Fallingbostel

We should have known why we got the full parcels. A day or two later the announcement was posted on the board. We were to be prepared to move on short notice!

One of the German guards told us the Russians were moving in our direction. When we moved out, the Prison Camp would be destroyed, even the Red Cross parcels. Nothing would be left for the Russians.

At noon the next day, we were on our way. A sorry-looking lot we were, with everything we owned on our backs and a Red Cross parcel under one arm. It took hours to clear a camp this large. Fortunately, Cam and I were away fairly soon. As it turned out, this was a very bad march. Most of the boys were getting the "screamers," a deadly situation because they had to take off their back packs to relieve themselves, and all that fuss and bother made things even worse. We had several kilometres to march, and the guards were getting tough. The dogs didn't help. Some Kriegies couldn't cope and left all their possessions at the side of the road — everything! They were just too sick with dysentery to care.

We heard gunfire very close to us and, when we arrived at the siding, the train engine was still leaking steam. It had been attacked and hit by a Russian aircraft, and was a write-off. The Germans told us to put our baggage in a boxcar. The P.O.W.'s would be returned to Thorn.

157

When I heard this, I volunteered to guard the luggage and, when the Germans agreed, I got Cam to stow both of our kit bags near the loading doors. With his bad foot, he didn't want to get stranded on his own and decided to stick with the others even with the march back, which he felt should be easy without baggage. He assured me his own insides were in pretty good shape. I had another R.A.F.-type staying with me, plus a German guard to whom I had already explained the value in having our own baggage near the door. If there was another air attack, we might have to take off but, if not, we could boil up a cup of coffee on our little blower.

We went out of our way to assure the guard we were not interested in taking off because we were responsible for all the baggage and asked him to leave the doors open. I promised to make him a real, honest-to-god cup of coffee, if it was possible later on. He hadn't had one of those for years.

A train pulled up on a siding just across from us. It was all boxcars just like ours but, when the doors were opened, we could see that each car had German soldiers lying on the floor swathed in a kind of paper bandage that I had never seen before.

I talked to the nearest orderly and was surprised to find that most of them, all Russian prisoners, spoke English. The severely wounded men were apparently Germans returning from the Russian Front.

I set up the blower, found some scraps of paper and wood, and started a fire. Then I opened the coffee tin and let the guard smell it. That was bribery! After that, there was no problem getting water, why he even volunteered to get it.

I must admit, I was making a production out of this, but the coffee was ground and sealed, and when it went in the water, that beautiful aroma came up. Jake, my Kreigie mate, dug out some sugar and powdered milk and lined up the three mugs. We got about two-thirds of a mug each.

The guard thought he had died and gone to heaven! Jake and I then opened our Red Cross parcels and made a sandwich using our bread ration, but with real butter and sardines. We probably set German morale back ten years with that exhibition! Even the Russians were watching.

After supper, the Russians came a little closer. Then came the sentence I have never forgotten.

"Are you a millionaire?"

I wasn't too sure how to answer this since I didn't know what constituted a millionaire to them, and then it dawned on me. He had seen my Canada flashes which I had pinned on the American flying jacket. They believed that in North America everybody was a millionaire! Compared to their lot in life, we were millionaires for sure!

That evening, we had other visitors, but the guard wouldn't let them get too close. One of them had a certain amount of appeal, since she was available for half a cake of soap. Jake and I gave this some thought, but decided if she need the soap that badly, we had better leave her alone. We did have our own little laugh about bouncing around on the baggage. We didn't lack imagination.

The morning brought no sign of our Kreigies, so we closed the doors and the guard took us up front to have a look at the engine. There wasn't much of the boiler left. The Russian fighter must have gotten a direct hit. It had already been pulled off the track and the track repaired. The guard told us a new engine would be hooked on that afternoon. On the way back, we passed the station and got permission to use the washroom, telling the guard to fill his water bottle so we could make coffee again before his relief came on.

The hospital train was off-loading some of the men, those that didn't make it, I assumed. They were put onto vans and the stretchers were returned. There wasn't a darn thing we could do about that. We just went about our own business but, German or not, we couldn't help but feel sorry for the useless loss of life.

Our guard was standing very close, we noticed, as we waited for the coffee to boil up. So, once again, we laid out the three cups, cut a slice of bread each for Jake and me and found the can of strawberry and apple jam. We offered the jam to the guard, but told him to use his own bread and margarine, which he did in a hurry. His ration was not much bigger than ours, since he was not on the front line!

Our boys were walking in slowly, with no semblance of order

159

at all. They must have had a terrible trip. When Cam arrived, I got him to climb up in the car. I showed him where our stuff was stored and told him to stay close to it because all the others would be after their own baggage. Judging by the look of them, I doubted that they could climb up. I then made Cam a coffee and heard his story.

The Germans had got rough with them and wouldn't let them stop when they had to go. This, of course, just made the matter worse. Most of them had left all their possessions at the train and couldn't even get a glass of water. But dysentery was the main problem. Some of them found their own kit that they had dumped on the way out and rescued their food. Cam had been smart enough to take back his mug and some travel rations. When they returned to camp, they found that everything had been ransacked. Once again, they rummaged through and found the odd item of use. They organized a squad and asked permission to go to the Red Cross depot. Twelve men and two guards were allowed out, but there was a limit to what they could bring back even with a four-wheeled cart. By morning they were very hungry.

They started out again by noon, but had to go so very slowly. Half the boys were bleeding now, but they were afraid to stay behind. They were not certain how far the Gerries would go, and had good reason to be fearful.

They came to the boxcar to find their kit, but this took time. There were hundreds of bags and boxes to sort. Jake and I called out names and handed them down, as two more boys came up to help.

Once they had their kit, they were assigned to a boxcar and were stuck in there for good. We kept Cam's inside the car, out of sight, so that we wouldn't get separated. With fighter plane activity in the area, we expected to start out at dusk. Again, this was against the Geneva Convention which stated, "No transportation of Prisoners of War after Sundown." There were a dozen boxes and bags left unclaimed, so we had them transferred to the nearest boxcar for sorting at our destination. Cam and I headed for a boxcar ourselves. They were set up the same way as on our last trip with three components separated with barbed wire. I had filled up all the containers we had with water. This was quite a balancing act.

We did start moving at dusk, which saved us a long wait. It

would not be a very good trip though. Dysentery was with us even before we started. Two of our boys who spoke German had a talk with our guards and explained how dangerous this was both to them and to us. They also explained that sanitation was most important, that the buckets must be emptied every day, that the buckets must be rinsed every day, and that a pail of water on hand would help. They also mentioned that the war would be over soon and a friend or two on the other side might be wise.

It was now November, 1944. It was sometimes difficult to get through to the average German just what was happening. Their propaganda was so persuasive that they believed it. They knew nothing about the total war. They did know, however, that the Russians were getting close and they were getting nervous. We were also getting a little nervous.

Our destination was Fallingbostel, a large Air Force P.O.W. camp near Hanover. We would be back in the heart of Germany, and the centre of the aerial war zone.

After a full day on the train, things were a real mess and the second day was worse. By the third day, we were pleading for a half hour stopover anywhere, anytime! Either that, or we would lose some men with dysentery. This time, I guess, we got through. The train shunted onto a spur line, the guards surrounded a field and let us out. Fresh air can be so very precious!

On the fourth day, we saw our new home for the first time. With Winter coming on, Cam and I moved fast to locate our bunk near the cooking/heating stove. Again, I got an upper with Cam below. The building we were in was a one storey pig farm with ten rooms, each one about one hundred and fifty feet front to back, and thirty feet across. It was constructed of cinder blocks and looked dull as hell.

Two single, sixty-watt bulbs were our only source of light when the doors were closed. These bulbs hung from the rafters, each on a single wire and socket. An exciting decor! At least they were hung near the stove. There were some small cuttings from constructing bunk frames which I gathered up as quickly as possible for blower fuel, and I even found a couple of nails. Nothing went to waste. Old newspapers were worth their weight in gold.

We were fortunate we had been able to transport all our

161

"gear." We had used a two gallon dhobe bucket to transport our utensils, taking turns carrying it. Our most valuable communal possession had been carried out in a football and was reported to be safe and working fine. That, of course, was the camp radio.

If the routine was the same at this camp, the Gerries would call a roll call on the parade grounds out front of the hut, then conduct a search inside the rooms. With the search in mind, we took anything valuable or contraband with us. And that's exactly what happened. The only damage this time was that they had dumped my neatly stacked little wood pile. We lost a few tools and knives collectively, but nothing of ours was taken. They then announced the straw pile and burlap bags had arrived to make our own mattresses.

I'm quite sure these bags or sacks were there all the time, but it made it easier for the goons (Gerries) to search the rooms without the bags lying across the bedboards.

The next morning, I went on the circuit looking for a Russian contact, and I found one. He was one of many that I have described before, a civilian labourer captured in Russia and marched into Germany as a slave. He was one of my "survivors," the same as at Barth. They were afraid of going back to Russia and would rather live the life they had!

He instinctively knew I wanted to trade and then he wandered over to the goon in the box overhead and made his own private deal. When he returned, I said "brott." I did not speak German, but had a few essential words. I wanted a loaf of bread. Then I added "morgen" (morning) and showed him a pack of cigarettes before turning and walking away.

The next morning, I stretched out on the grass and waited. Before long, a loaf of bread plunked down near me, a big brown loaf shaped like a football. I got up and spun a packet of cigarettes over the fence. The Russian held up two fingers. I shook my head and grinned. He lifted his shoulders in a shrug and grinned back. I picked up the loaf, put it under my jacket, and walked back to the hut. There was more bread in that loaf than our two rations for one week combined! Cam asked if we had sold the farm! I wondered to myself how many cigarettes the guard got — or did he get them all?

With prisoners coming in daily from several of the other camps to the east, our P.O.W. camp was growing by leaps and bounds. We were sure that the Russian push must have been on a very wide front. New boys coming in directly from OPS did not figure the war would last another three months even, and news by radio was most upbeat. The Allies were moving!

Mail from home was finally coming in, and this included cartons of cigarettes mailed directly to us. The price for a loaf of bread would be going up again after this influx. Most of these incoming letters had been written three months ago, and now it was two weeks from Christmas and nobody had yet sent greetings to any of the boys. They would probably arrive in February.

We were keeping busy building a drainage pipe out of tin cans. Since we were on a bit of a slope down the length of our building, the pipe would work like a weeping tile bed and keep us a little drier in winter.

Some boxing matches were organized. There would be three bouts, each boxer fighting for three, one minute rounds. On their low caloric intake, it was impossible to go longer. The boxers were given one week to train, and the bookmakers immediately went into action. The excitement this created was unbelievable.

An English policeman by the name of Nicholson was favoured for the heavies, but certainly not through personality. He was intensely disliked by many. So much for the London bobbies. The second match would be between Ginger Parkes and Burglar Bill, and we expected it to be a dandy. The third bout had Tony Johnson from our own room against an unknown. Tony was new at this, but was being trained by Burglar Bill and was declared to be very good.

On the day of the fights, we put out four chairs facing away from the ring and four men straddled them backwards. This gave us the chair backs to tie the ropes (actually just pieces of string) to. The floor was hard sand, and the gloves worn were the large gym type supplied by the Red Cross. The referee did have a whistle, and the bell was a dish pan and spoon. First class all the way!

The fights were called for the afternoon at a time clear of the daily roll calls. Since seats for all were not available, most of the Kreigies sat on the ground. The announcer put on a real act of introducing each fighter and listed their former wins, including their girlfriends and the doorman at Kelly's Bar and Beanery.

The first two rounds of the first fight made for quite a slugging match. The third round was comical as hell because, before long, neither fighter could lift his arms anymore, and it became a flat-footed dance with no orchestra. Well, that's not quite true. The fans supplied the music at no charge.

The second fight was a beaut, more fencing than slugging. They paced themselves and lasted well. Burglar Bill won that fight, but not by very much.

Tony Johnson was an easy winner in the third fight. He used a straight out punch from the shoulder and got through his opponent's defence several times. Here it is, fifty years later, and I still remember those fights like it was yesterday.

I kept in contact with my Russian friend, and one day settled for a good sized cabbage. Cam made a stew, after giving about a third of the cabbage to other boys in the hut. There was always the hope they would reciprocate when able.

In the past few months, our news reports had indicated that an attempt on Hitler's life by his own senior officers had failed; that the British attempt to sweep through Holland had been stopped with heavy loss of life at Arnheim; that "HOME for CHRISTMAS" was a dead duck this year; and that the long sweep into France from the sea was ever more successful — but boy, did we get restless! We knew now that we would win the war eventually.

The guards had no permissible access to B.B.C. broadcasts, but we were eager to pass on the good news. Their reaction to the information varied widely. The older guards, many of them First World War vets, were quite resigned to the ultimate outcome. The Hitler Youth, however, just didn't believe us. Since their earliest years, they had been led to believe they were members of the MASTER race and, probably for a lifetime, would suffer from the delusion. In the meantime, they were proper bastards! They were cruel vicious punks but, worse still, they had been trained to be that way!

I had lost track of the other members of my crew since our last moves and was trying hard to trace them, but thus far had had no luck. I believed they might have been transferred with the others just before going to Poland.

It was lucky for me I had bartered for that Yankee flying jacket. Winter was setting in pretty fast and, although there was not much snow, it was bitterly cold. The walls and the floors of the huts were continually wet with condensation, because of the moisture that built up when the doors were closed on us at nights and the lack of cross ventilation. Ice often formed on the inner walls. There was a little relief when the stove was used for cooking. Our stove at this time was a wide, flat top, wood and coal burner. We did not get a wood ration though, and were relying on our one briquette per man, per day. When the briquette supply became critical in January, we were granted permission to go on a work party and bring back as much wood as we could carry. This was not very much on an individual basis, but it all went into the same stove and added up to considerable heat.

By Christmas, Red Cross parcels were not reaching us, so we were down to our basic two potatoes and three slices of black bread per day, plus one bowl of barley each week. The cigarette supply was also getting so tight that trades over the wire were down to the "ten cigarette level" for a loaf of bread. Cam had saved up a couple of cans of meat for special occasions. I decided to write "February 1st, 1945" on a few pieces of paper and pin them up everywhere, since that would be my twenty-fourth birthday.

My birthday arrived at the same time as our Christmas mail. Better late than never! We especially enjoyed those Mackenzie King greeting cards wishing us a "Happy Christmas!" Such an opportunity for a politician to miss! We realized that our Prime Minister did not have a clue about our ordeal.

The fact that our Red Cross parcels were not reaching us was also maddening, since they were being stored less than a mile from our camp. The Gerries said they didn't have the transportation available. And they were the ones with the guns?

By February, a huge tent city was building up in a new compound over from us. There must have been one thousand new men there already. We were waiting for someone to fill us in on the details. Finally, two Americans from the new lager came over and shot the bull for a while. They told us the fences between had been removed, and that there were some R.A.F. types over there now. Maybe our own buddies from Hydekrug! There were ten full length sections in our building, and three of them were still empty, so if these men turned out to be our friends, we hoped they would be permitted to transfer from the tents.

I checked with my Russian friend at the wire, then kept on going until I reached the tents. It was a long walk with some mud in the field to get through. At the tents, they directed me to the R.A.F. section.

There were about one hundred R.A.F. over there and many of them were Canadians. Some of these boys had been at Barth with us. When I told them about the empty bunks in our section, they really reacted and said they would look into it right away. I mentioned that Dixie might be able to arrange the transfer, and that I would contact him as soon as I returned to my compound. These boys hadn't seen him for well over a year, and had not had a very good time of things lately with no camp leader to speak for them. The Russians, by the way, were right behind them when they left.

Sometimes we could see our bombers in the searchlights, bombing cities to the north of us, and we occasionally saw further daylight bombing raids directly overhead. The Americans were in huge formations. The big news, however, came in on the radio. Not only were we advancing again, but the Russians had crossed the eastern frontier of Germany.

A shout came at us that Canadians were marching in. Although, marching is hardly the word. These men looked completely exhausted. It didn't take us long to realize that these were our own bunch who had broken off between Hydekrug and Thorn. They had ended up on an island in the Baltic near Swinemunde. For the past thirty days, as far as I could gather, they had been on the road marching westward. I spotted Pat Hoag and got him to the hut and made a fast brew while Cam looked for a slice of bread. Fortunately, we had a few cigarettes for him. While Cam talked to him, others began to show up. These weren't just friends, these were our very good friends — Pop Kingdon, Ted Bundy, Stu Saunders, Ab Rey and Daby Dabous. In fact, there were so many of them and so many years

166

had passed, I got confused as to which ones came back and which were already with us from Thorn.

While all this was going on, I went to the fence area where I might find my Russian friend, hoping to get a loaf of bread. He signalled to return in one hour. I followed his instructions; the guard nodded and over came the bread; back went a package of cigarettes; with a fast wave, off I went. We cut the loaf in slices, spread it with margarine, and wrapped a third of the loaf in Pat's dirty shirt. I felt like a benevolent grandmother.

It was so damp and cold in the rooms that we either lived around the stove or were out on the blower burning up our bedboards. But Cam, the crafty sod, had built a hammock of string over his bed frame and didn't need all his bedboards.

A surprise Gestapo raid changed all this. Alas, they cut through Cam's strings with a jack knife and left him with nothing. Further, as a reprisal, they took two bedboards off each bunk. That left most of us with two. What the reprisal was for, we never did find out. All we knew was that two, five inch wide bedboards would not support a straw mattress.

Not to be beaten, Cam sewed up his one and only blanket into a sleeping bag and suggested I do the same. Now that was some feat for me but, being a very kind, considerate person, I went along with the gag. We then put the four bedboards on one bunk with the two sleeping bags. In the morning, my rump was on the ground and Cam was in a precarious suspension above me. He had taken back his two bedboards just because I had nearly kicked his teeth out. We had been sleeping with my head at one end and his at the other, and I guess in my sleep temptation had been too great.

No one would believe the stories about the Gestapo unless they had seen them. Although they were Hitler's secret police force, they were not in military uniform. They, however, all dressed alike with black, horsehide jacket coats and black, wide-rimmed fedoras. I remember them best, not for their vicious acts or their complete lack of humour, but for their stupid, although sinister, appearance. How could these people ever come to power? I find that an easy question to answer. In our complacency, we are allowing them to practise right now! Right in Canada!

167

Right in the U.S.A.! Right in Britain! And even in Germany, where the poor simple souls are allowing their sons to join the Nazi Party all over again. When is our own government going to step on these dangerous punks?!

Every misguided kid they recruit will be an enemy of our own government and that means you, Mr. Politician!

We outlawed them before. Let's do it again. NOW! And, don't talk to me about freedom. I fought for freedom.

February passed, and another birthday went by. All sports were at a standstill, and the only thing that mattered was the daily news. It was still winter, but Cam and I walked the mile-long circuit, just to escape from the close quarters of our hut. Dixie had advised us not to try escaping from Fallingbostel if the war continued in our favour, as things were becoming very unsettled outside the camp. The guards were very touchy. Even the laughs on the parades were falling off.

One of our boys, still in his twenties but looking much younger, achieved fame through food poisoning after less than three months as a prisoner of war. Who would have ever predicted that a boy like this would hold a National Record? We suspected he had not yet been taken by the hand and taught to express himself. First of all, his lips began to swell. I don't mean a little, but oh, you know, like a Ubangi. Yes, that's it. Just like a Ubangi! But there was no prize for that. It was the next item that made his claim for fame and fortune.

Of all things, his you-know-whats began to swell. At walnut size, they never attracted attention and, as baseballs, they were better than average but, as grapefruit, they were magnificent. There were problems, however. He couldn't get up without getting embarrassed. He was terrified of sitting down. The line ups to have a peek at this phenomenon got longer and longer, and eventually began to bother him. He threatened to cover up, but any clothing that made contact was quickly removed. There was only one thing to do — build a large-sized jewel box to put them in so that nothing interfered. A shoe box was perfect and old socks did well for padding, although he did have to get used to lying down at a wide angle.

Three days later, the swelling disappeared with no trace. All

168

plans to sell tickets were soon forgotten. The shoe box, however, was hung with pride above his headboard.

With war fronts both to the east and to the west, it was a wonder that we received mail at all. Fortunately, all our mail was cleared through the Red Cross from Switzerland to the south and Sweden to the north. Married men, about five per cent of the Canadians in the Air Force P.O.W. camps and about twenty per cent of the British, were the ones who missed the mail the most. It must have been terrible to have little children at home and no regular contact. The fiancees' letters, however, were public property.

"You didn't say you loved me in your last letter, so I married Sam."

"I know Berlin is a big city, but my cousin lives there. Why don't you pop over. She's easy to spot. She's a blonde."

Early in March, with news getting really good, a big shipment of Red Cross parcels came in the gates amidst loads of cheers. I had a theory on this and predicted we were moving out soon.

The same thing had happened twice before — it wasn't so much a gift as a cover up. If the Red Cross checked on their warehouses and found undistributed parcels after the camp was vacated, they would raise Cain. Gerry would try to avoid this, since the trouble went over their heads at the camp level. Our present offering amounted to a parcel for every two men, and nobody argued.

Our friends from the island told us quite a rough story. They had been marched from the train siding to a ship loading dock in the Baltic, then put in the hold of a freighter. It was cold, dark, wet, and crowded. They were down there for several days until they landed on the island. Then things got worse. Their guards were German Navy and tough as hell. They hand-cuffed our boys in pairs and made them run the gauntlet on the double between fixed bayonets, and used them often.

Most of the information in my story is first-hand. In this case, that verification is not possible, but I knew the principals well enough to believe every word. I feel that it is important to tell of this episode here, since there are many who have never heard it before. Walter (Pat) Hoag of Picton, a friend for so many years, was the first one to stumble into our hut with the information. Several boys counted over a dozen jabs that day, where the guards had pierced their skins. Resistance was impossible and, yet, there were a few courageous cases we heard about. Sherry, a former boxer from British Columbia, held off a guard's bayonet, but was hit over the head by another guard and brought to his knees. The rifle butt broke, but Sherry staggered up again and carried on.

The radio reports now were just amazing. The British were fighting in Germany and sweeping to the north and east. The Russians were also in Germany and heading towards Berlin. The Americans and other Allies were advancing from the south in a broad sweep. Surely it wouldn't be long now.

- CHAPTER 21 -

Fallingbostel is Evacuated

Suddenly, we were given our orders to evacuate the camp at Fallingbostel. Cam and I had done some preparation for this and would not try to carry all our possessions. Our troops were only about two hundred miles away. There were no static front lines anymore. The advances seemed to be "break through" and "fast advances." We also seemed to dominate the skies, which added a great deal of danger.

We headed south and east to start. We were given a bread ration of a third of a loaf of black bread each, and that was it. There were thousands of us. The guards tried to move us faster by siccing the dogs on us from the rear. We received no more food for a week, but stole what we could from the fields, mostly turnips or swedes, which were coarser and used for cattle feed. Dysentery was back once again, with a vengeance. At nights we slept where we could. I found that a towel over my head gave me the warmth I needed. I slept right on the road the first night.

A few of the boys had built four-wheel carts to carry their loads, and took turns pushing the carts. It took four men, two to push and two more to keep putting the wooden wheels back on.

The next day, we changed direction and swung to the north. There were no military vehicles on this road, but aircraft were low overhead. By afternoon, we were all exhausted and a German officer commandeered a huge barn for us to sleep in.

At the barn, the first place I headed for was the chicken feed. Others headed for the chickens. Half a pot of this seed was a failure as the oats still had their husks on.

At about four in the morning, Allison, another Toronto boy, said, "Let's look for eggs. I know all about chickens."

The guards, all older, First War vets, were asleep in the ditch so we quietly stepped over them and headed for the next farm house. Allison said, "We will steal what we can. You bang on the front door and I'll sneak in the back door." I waited and waited and was getting nervous when the door finally opened.

It was Allison! "What do you want?" he asked.

We spotted a huge hen house next door and sneaked over. "You stand guard," he said, "I'll get the eggs." There were a helluva lot of squawks coming from the hens inside but, finally, out came Allison with his shirt bulging with eggs. "Nothing to it," he boasted.

We sneaked back over the guards who were so tired they might never wake up. We sat down to divvy up the eggs. There were no eggs — all layer dummies. So much for knowledgable partners! Maybe he just went after the hard boiled ones.

Some of our men got hold of the German officer in charge of the march and reminded him that we had not been given any rations for five days. They asked permission to slaughter some farmers' cows. The officers refused, but pointed to a young heifer they could have. They couldn't feed the multitude with that one, but we weren't about to turn down anything! They called for a volunteer butcher. That's when they learned we had one thousand butchers in our compound.

The next day was a major disaster to all British Air Force prisoners of war. A flight of Typhoons spotted us and mistook us for German troops. They started ahead of the column and ripped down the middle of the entire length. Cam and I were near the rear and I just made the ditch in time for a Gerry guard to pile on top of me. As we climbed out of the ditch, I noticed one of the planes doing a tight turn not far behind us. I hollered, "He's coming in again." That was not to be. He was too low and too tight. His wing tip hit the ground on his turn to port, he cartwheeled and burst into flames. Then, there was a big explosion!

172

From where we were located, it took us a while to get the facts, but two names stood out in the long list of men killed that day. Zeke Fox, our former combine mate, and Jock Durnan, one of the most popular men in camp, had both been killed. Zeke had been helping to push a four-wheel cart when he was hit. Jock, who had worked in our camp kitchen for years, was lying down on the straw in the big barn. Pop Kingdon was evidently right beside Jock, but survived. It was an indescribably awful feeling to know these were our own planes firing at us with cannon shells, and we had no way to stop them.

- CHAPTER 22 -

Escape

That raid had made me very restless. I talked to Cam about escaping since they were neither protecting nor feeding us. Cam felt it best for him to stay with the column because of his banged up foot, and I agreed with him that he couldn't run if it became necessary. I decided to take off on my own. I turned all our communal food over to Cam, as I felt I could steal some as I went along.

Both the guards and the dogs were becoming indifferent so it wasn't too difficult to get away. When we passed through a forest, I slipped away and ran like hell for ten minutes, then found a hiding place. For two hours, I stayed still and listened, then got up and headed in the general direction of the noise I could hear.

When I reached a wide road with tractor treads on it, I backed off fifty yards and laid down to rest until dark. Then it dawned on me that those were not tractor treads, those were tank treads. While resting, two men I knew came close by. One was Gus Mortson from Greencourt, Alberta, along with a boy named Bob from Vancouver. I must have given them quite a start when I called to them. They wanted no part of company and took off again. That suited me fine.

I travelled carefully after dusk, keeping to the shadows, and heading in what I felt was the right direction. I had no problems, just a couple of scares from what were probably birds in the trees nearby. After a couple of hours, I became tired and headed back

174

into an open field and promptly fell asleep. I awoke at dawn and walked back into some trees nearby. Once again, I fell asleep but awakened feeling uneasy. My eyes opened to find a deer looking down at me. When I sat up, she jumped back a few feet and continued to stare at me. Nearby were three other deer, two of them very small and spotted. When the initial surprise wore off, I said to myself, "This is silly. You have never been in a more dangerous position in your life, and you're worried about a deer!" I got up and she bounded away.

In my kit, there was a small, but very welcome, bottle of water. I had filled it twice before from streams and retrieved it now along with the last of my food. I knew I would have to find a farm house soon. Although it was still daylight, I headed out anyway in the same general direction I had been going. Two more of our boys showed up, doing a lousy job of hiding themselves. One was George Williams from Toronto. The other, nicknamed Lofty, was an R.A.F.-type whose last name escapes me. We were soon in an argument over direction, and I thought, "Not for me." Lofty kept announcing himself as a born leader. He also kept passing out.

Suddenly, what turned out to be a flame thrower opened up not two hundred yards away and scared the hell out of me. I headed for a stream nearby and jumped in. The water wasn't nearly as tough on me as the nettles were when I got out. I didn't care if the whole Nazi Army came at me; I had never experienced an itch like that before. It took me half and hour to settle down.

What happened to the others no longer mattered, and I headed out, blisters and all. Farther down the road, there was a farm house set well back. Rather than follow the road, I crossed a field where some children spotted me and ran into the nearby house. About five minutes later, the farmer came out and walked directly towards me and called out in English, "Are you a prisoner?"

I answered, "Yes."

He then replied, "Come to the house."

George and Lofty were ahead of me. The farmer asked if we would like some milk. With the three little children staring at us from the doorway, I felt like the bogey man!

He told us the English had just been there, and he would

Beaupre and friend
in POW camp at Sagan

guide us to their bivouac. The farmer did not seem at all afraid of us, so our soldiers must have been O.K. towards him. We headed out before it got too dark and walked about a mile. Lofty passed out once again, so we had to wait for a little while. We were on a sandy road and I was one hundred feet ahead of the others, when suddenly a voice called out, "Halt or I'll shoot."

My reply was just a cryptic, "For Christ's sake, don't shoot. We're Canadians."

"One only advance. O.K. stop right there," was their response.

I quickly interjected and calmly said, "Air Force P.O.W.'s".

The soldiers said, "O.K. Keep on this road for about a mile. You will see our camp. Ask for the Officer of the Day."

I asked him to let the farmer go since he had guided us there. There was no sign of Lofty. Maybe he had passed out again.

The soldier called after me, "Don't leave the road."

The first thing I saw when I reached the camp was the cook house with an armoured vehicle pulled up beside it. There were two soldiers sitting on the grass beside the cook house. My clothing didn't reveal much, but they guessed I was a P.O.W., so I filled them in. One of them asked, "Want some grub?"

"Sure do," I replied.

"How about some bacon and eggs?"

"Geez," I said, "I haven't seen a real live egg in years!"

"How many?" I was asked.

"Three," I answered.

"Where is your billy can?" he asked.

"I don't have one," I answered. "Put it on bread".

Three eggs on a slice of bread — white bread — didn't leave much space. With bacon, it left no space at all. "Put the lid on!" I said. I then sank to the floor with this glorious mess on my lap.

I took my mug off my belt and he said, "Never seen one like that before."

"Got it from my Russian grandfather."

"Oh," he grunted. When he filled my mug with real live coffee, I could have cried.

The others were coming in, and Lofty made it after all. The other soldier offered me a drink, then took me out to a vehicle which turned out to be an ammunition carrier with big trays on either side. He lifted the lid on every tray down one side. I didn't see any ammunition, but every tray was loaded with bottles of booze commandeered from the pub in the last city they went through. No beer, just spirits. So, he handed me a bottle.

I washed my bacon and eggs down with some of whatever that foreign label read, and cooled it all off with coffee, which was still scalding because of the metal cup. That bread tasted just like cake, I thought to myself.

The soldier got me a rifle along with a clip of shells. He told me to sleep on the straw in the barn. "Don't shoot the goat," he warned, "That's our mascot."

It was just as well I was forewarned about the goat. It was making retching noises and belching all the time I was in the barn. However, the white bread was not sitting too well, and it wasn't too long before I was out-belching the goat. I don't know whether I fell asleep or passed out, but it didn't seem long before a shout rang out. A jeep was waiting for us. He was going into town, a mile back, and could drop us off.

The jeep took off with a German P.O.W. sitting on the hood as a look out for aircraft. When a low flying aircraft headed our way, the jeep stopped, and everyone headed for the ditch. I had a good look at the aircraft. Big nose, but no prop. "FW190," they said. I had just seen my first jet! Faster than a speeding bullet.

The duty officer in the village took us over one by one into a vacant room containing nothing but a chair and a table, a pad of paper and a bottle of booze. He offered me a glass of whisky but, at seven o'clock in the morning, it had lost its appeal. Then he said, "You don't mind if I do?"

Feeling big hearted, I said, "No."

He took down my name, number and rank. He then asked me what a Flight Sergeant was. "In Canada," I said, "it's one higher than a Sergeant. In the R.A.F., it's one lower than a Private." "Well," he said, "we will let the next son-of-a-bitch finish this. You're safe here, except for snipers. We only took this town yesterday. Sure you don't want a drink? Some time today, we'll take you to an evacuation camp. We're short of men. Would you mind standing guard on one of our own P.O.W.'s? We would like a hole made to dump the garbage in." These were front line soldiers, British 7th Armoured Division.

This poor, bewildered, P.O.W. didn't speak English. By the features, I would guess he was Slavic. But he was in German uniform, which gave him some protection. One of our soldiers gave him a spade and took off. I took the spade and marked off a hole wider than the spade was long. The poor guy thought it was longer than it was wide, and that I was going to shoot and bury him. I pointed to the garbage and, in pantomime, I dropped it in. His head began to bob up and down, and a happy smile showed through the tears. He went to work like a demon. After all, they were probably feeding him whisky for breakfast, too!

An hour later, a lorry pulled up with a half dozen Kriegies in it. We piled on board. Once again, we had a German P.O.W. sitting on board as look out! We were heading to an evacuation camp. They must have liked this name, they used it often. "Where was this camp?" we asked. "At a town called Fallingbostel." This made some of us laugh, since we had just left Fallingbostel several weeks ago as P.O.W.'s. Now, it had been liberated, and we were returning there to await transport to Brussels for a flight home. The other men on the lorry were soldiers doing forced labour on farms nearby.

We had mixed feelings about returning to Fallingbostel, but the weather was getting better and the doors could be left open in the huts. Some of our boys were back there, but many were not, and we hoped they were free and on their way to Brussels. I couldn't find Cameron.

That afternoon, I sat on a hillside just inside the main gate which was now wide open. I was one of at least one hundred others watching the best side show in town — courtesy of the Welsh guards, if my memory serves me correctly.

They had ordered the town council to report to the main gates of our camp in formal regalia. When they were all there and a good crowd had gathered, they were each handed a shovel and told to dig a latrine ditch.

The mayor started out with his silk topper and morning coat, but soon he was down to his shirt sleeves. The soldiers made him keep on his ribbon and medal of office. It sat so proudly on that

179

tummy of his. All the time, our boys were cheering and clapping. We were told this was the man who could have arranged delivery of our Red Cross parcels from the warehouse in town.

The army opened a kitchen for us. We could have as much as we liked, as often as we liked, but nobody could really eat much volume. Our stomachs had shrunk, and we didn't handle rich foods too well. But, it sure was fun trying. The results, however, for the first few days were disastrous.

More and more Kriegies were arriving from all directions, and soon there were thousands in the camp. A command post was established with a bulletin board. The rules were simple. You wrote your name, number and rank on the embarkation list, and waited. Each morning, a convoy of ten army lorries drove in and picked up those men whose names appeared at the top of the list. We were told to leave behind most of our clothing, as it would be burned in Brussels and replaced with army uniforms. It would be a long trip.

While waiting, which we were told would be a few days, we were free to do what we pleased, inside or outside the camp. A new camp leader had to be appointed every day because first thing, as a new camp leader, he would mark himself in for tomorrow's draft.

One day, my old friend Yakov, the Russian fence trader, showed up with his tall, thin friend. When he saw me, he came over. He didn't look so hot, but he could still grin. He indicated they were hungry, so I took them to the hut and made them the damnedest sandwich you ever saw. I told them to sit outside and wait. I couldn't leave them inside too long because they had body lice. When they were finished eating, I took them to the detox centre for delousing, and then lined up a Red Cross parcel for them. They were starving, all right!

The next day, I heard about that big, big building everyone called the "magasin," which had looked so out of place in a prisoner of war camp. We had always wondered what was inside. With the Germans gone, we soon found out. It was full of contra-band merchandise from France. The French stores had been stripped of valuable merchandise, and the goods sent to this central warehouse for distribution to the chosen few. One whole floor was taken up with perfumes.

The Russian ex-slaves were the first to raid it. There was only one sensible thing to do with very expensive cologne. Drink it! Of course, what else?

The next obvious thing they found to do was get hold of a pair of Verie pistols and cartridges that were abandoned and fight a duel. The one who died was buried in the camp. His mate was so drunk, he didn't even know what he had done. A phosphorus burn is maybe the worst known way to go. One of our survivors didn't make it! Six years of war and then this!

On yet another day, these Russians learned about motorcycles. The British Army topped up the tanks on some abandoned machines, sat a Russian on the seat, and showed him how to drive. They even gave him a push start, but they forgot to tell him how to stop. Most of them walked back. One of them rode for a whole kilometre before breaking his arm. He marched in, sans cycle, laughing the whole time! Best fun he had had in a whole lifetime! An army orderly set his arm.

The one thing Russian survivors were good at, very good at indeed, was the art of sifting through a garbage pail looking for food. At present, we fed them anything they wanted, but they knew that when we were gone, they would have to revert to the garbage pails, or look for some other way of feeding themselves.

Although they were free, and the war with Germany would be surely over soon, they couldn't go back to their native Russia. The Russians looked upon them as traitors for working for the Germans. They were truly men without a country.

Our turn was not far off now. We would leave for Brussels and, then, a flight back to Britain. The R.C.A.F. had sent Canadian officers to interview us. They were to submit a report on each of us as to our general health, our attitude and our plans. We noticed they didn't ask what we thought of Mackenzie King.

My own interviewer was the first to laugh. He had already been told about the Christmas card. He explained some of our options. Take our honourable discharge with full benefits, remain in the service, or volunteer for Far East service, since the Japanese War was still going strong. The majority of us would head home. Five years was enough!

- CHAPTER 23 -

To Brussels by Lorry, Then to England

It was April 19, 1945, when we got our turn on the Lorry. The journey took many hours, but we were fascinated by what we saw along the way. Thousands of people were on the move trying to head home. If they could find home! Every mode of transport was in use. Baby carriages were very popular, even children's wagons.

During a break along the way, the driver told us they were on the road fourteen hours every day in order to get the boys home. Yesterday, one driver had gone off the road and was killed. He hit the ditch too hard and was pinned behind the wheel.

We pulled in to the barracks in Brussels later that afternoon and immediately called for pay parade. That caused a laugh!

We were allocated a bed and then we were off to the showers and detox. Lots of towels were laid out, and plenty of razor blades and razors were handed out. Stoves were set up nearby with clothing issued on the spot. Last of all, uniforms. These were Army uniforms, and I was becoming more proud of our Army every minute. They must all have been six feet, nine inches! With the sleeves rolled up twice, I found my finger tips, which was comforting, since at first I thought I'd lost them! As far as the pants were concerned, a pair of scissors solved the problem!

When I got back to the barracks, the one comment I dreaded most was waiting for me. "What kept you?!" asked Cameron.

He had arrived in Brussels a few days ahead of me. As far as we could sort out, what was left of the marching column had been liberated and returned to Fallingbostel. He had left for Brussels a day or two before I arrived at Fallingbostel. Tough beans — he missed the famous Russian motorcycle team!

Nobody pushed us the next morning, except to tell us breakfast was at seven and pay parade at nine. Believe me, nobody missed that, especially with years of back pay coming.

"How long were you a P.O.W.? How much do you want?" Surely, no paymaster ever said that before. I asked for $100.00 in English pounds and $100.00 in Belgian francs. He didn't bat an eyelash. "Would you like to try for double?" I said to myself.

We were advised that we would be here for only about two days, so we didn't go too far away. We didn't have to go far. There were hundreds of bars. We even found a bar with girls in it. We were, however, looking for enthusiastic amateurs and didn't stay too long anywhere. On our next stop, I came across the most striking lounge I had ever seen. The crystal chandelier took up half the ceiling and was truly awe inspiring. Evidently, it was a former Royal residence, right in the downtown of Brussels. It turned out to be a meeting place for lots of office girls after work. Well, we weren't after work, but we were after girls. We met some nice girls who didn't mind us spending our pay cheque on them. It was good to be back in the saddle!

Our dunnage bags along, with all our personal clothing, had arrived from England, but there was nothing left in mine but the socks that had been hand-knitted with loving care. Every pair was at least three inches long after having been washed in boiling water. My shoes, slippers, and shirts had all been stolen.

In Brussels, we were in billets for Air Force personnel. There were also Army and Navy quarters. We were advised that, weather permitting, a flight of Lancasters would arrive tomorrow morning to fly us back to England. This caused some terrifying sensations inside me. I kept having vivid flashbacks of the last time I had flown in a Lancaster. Nic was at the controls on our last operation. Never once did he show fear, and yet, he must have known, as I did, what the outcome would be.

On our last day in Brussels, we spent a little time shopping

183

for items the British girls could not get, regardless of money — four tubes of lipstick and six pairs of nylons. Enough to start a war! When it came to size, we had some fun with the salesgirls as to what was "just right."

Our flight was uneventful. There were so many of us, we all had to sit along the sides on the floor of the plane. We could not see out of the plane except by taking turns, which we did regularly. I should have booked the rear turret and felt right at home.

There was a big surprise for us when we landed. The R.A.F. had brought in a whole vanload of Air Force women to greet us. They ran out and teamed up with a girl for every P.O.W. A hug and a kiss was surely the best welcome home! Every one of them was beautiful!

A train brought us the last fifty miles to Bournemouth and then, there we were, right back to where we had started, so many years before. There had been quite a commotion on the train when we boarded. They were calling out, "Make way for P.O.W.'s!" and turfing everybody out of the compartments. They neglected to say "British P.O.W.'s," and the civilians resented their giving priority to Germans. I couldn't blame them for their attitude. When the confusion was straightened out, everything went into reverse. They crowded around us, shaking hands and slapping backs. A very warm welcome, indeed!

A lorry picked us up and took us to R.C.A.F. headquarters, still at the Bath House. Living quarters were arranged, and Cam and I were able to double up. An interview was then held for each of us to tell us what schedule we would be following. They gave me enough money to get fitted for a Warrant Officer's uniform and I was handed an envelope containing Warrant Officer First Class badges which were to be stitched on. My first class warrant badge was backdated two-and-a-half years! This information had never caught up to me. A Warrant Officer First Class wore the same uniform as a Commissioned Officer, but with an arm badge instead of a sleeve stripe.

They also handed me rail passes for London and return, where I could shop for a uniform.

Next came the medicals, where so many of us, eager to just go home as soon as possible, reported that there was nothing
184

wrong with us. Everything we told them went on a statement which we signed. We never dreamed that our problems with the prison camps might not show up for years, or that we would someday regret our proud assertions of good health.

A new identification folder was issued and endorsed with the word "malnutrition." This entitled us to all the milk we wanted, and just about anything else we wanted from the menu. The enclosed photo would have qualified me for a Charles Atlas course. I went into uniform at 155 pounds, and this photo showed me at 127 pounds. Two months before leaving Fallingbostel, I had cut my hair back to about one-quarter inch all over, but it was now back in, twice as thick. It probably weighed twice as much as I did! Cam had always worn his hair short. I think it must have been a boyhood fear of growing too tall. Since he had to go to London for the same reasons, we booked out and headed for the big city.

- CHAPTER 24 -

Back in Uniform

Upon our arrival in London, the tailors told us a new uniform (complete with badges) would be ready at ten o'clock the next morning. Away we went, straight to the Universal Brasserie in Piccadilly for a laugh or two, and a pint or three. It was a wonderful feeling to be free! We didn't see one soul we knew, a dramatic change from our previous visits.

We stayed over in Russell Square that night, and we presented ourselves in the morning. They checked the fit, sold us shirts, socks and a belt, and, of course, an Air Force tie. For shoes, we had to go down the street. Then, it was back up to the tailors, since we had forgotten about the trench coat. By now, we were just about financially wiped out, even with the clothing allowance, so we decided to head back to Bournemouth. On the train we slept most of the way.

Next day, we went on pay parade, then later I phoned Beryl's office. Although she had been transferred back to London, a girl I talked to gave me a new number to reach her. Beryl seemed pleased and told me she would be in Bournemouth on Saturday, and we could meet at the afternoon dance. She even promised to bring a friend for Cam. That suited me fine.

Harold Beaupre was in Bournemouth now, and it was good to see him. After his return flight from Brussels, he had reported directly back to #83 Squadron. I guess this was the right thing to

186

do. When he returned, he was sporting a D.F.C. and the new rank of Flight Lieutenant. He had earned it!

Bo told me he was heading up to Glasgow to Stan MacFarlane's home next week. I promised to try to make it, since this would probably be our last get-together in England.

I asked Cam what his plans were. He said he would take the train to see his pilot's family. Most of Cam's crew had been killed. He agreed to meet with me in Uddingston where Aunt Jeannie still lived. Jeannie told me she would phone Toronto for me right away to let them know I was O.K. and that I would be home in about two month's time. If you ever have an Aunt, make sure it's Aunt Jeannie! God bless her!

In the meantime, we got down to some serious beer drinking in Bournemouth. Most of our buddies were arriving from Germany raring to go. They didn't last as long as they thought, though. Physically, we were no hell yet! I know that, in my own case, I was adding weight, but it wasn't muscle. My chin became part of my chest with no sign of my neck at all. Straight baby fat. It stayed that way for several weeks.

That was the week I met my next door neighbour. He was sitting on a lawn looking lower than a skunk's belly when I spotted him. Paul Johnston, who is about four or five years younger than myself, had just arrived off the boat with a new officer's uniform and a pilot's wing. He wanted desperately to get into combat before the war was over and, on top of that, he was embarrassed about outranking me. I told him it didn't bother me, as my lack of progress through the ranks was due to having been a prisoner of war. It had been so easy for them to forget us. We were easy to entertain, too. All they had to do was send us a Christmas card from Mackenzie King every four years. Paul was a fine boy. I hope he has done well.

When Saturday rolled around, we headed for the summer Pavilion, a very lovely place surrounded by acres of flower beds and shrubs, Air Force types, and pretty girls. You would have never guessed the war with Germany was still going on. Listening in on the talks around the dance floor, I learned that at least half the girls were on the stage in London, and every member of Aircrew was on his third tour. Cam and I wondered who loaned them the wings to wear, and just how many were on the payroll at the Windmill Theatre.

We had a wonderful day. When Beryl arrived, I must admit she took my breath away. She also took several other guys' breaths away, judging by their fast action in asking for a dance. Tough beans, Mac, she's booked! We danced for hours. I loved having her in my arms and, all the time, I was making it tougher for myself.

The girl that came along with Beryl was from her office. She was a good scout, and Cam seemed to get along with her. Beryl had made arrangements for them to stay at her old address in Bournemouth. That day went by so very fast.

The next day we met the girls again and just wandered around the park. We had tea at Bobby's Restaurant, where they filled a three tier plate with sweet cakes and charged for what was missing. I told Cam that I was fighting for my freedom, but he stayed out of that one. All very well for him, he had a girl back home.

The girls were heading back to London that night for work the following morning. I was glad Betty had come along. Alone with Beryl, I would have been a dead duck, even a willing dead duck! I knew now that I didn't want to make a commitment. My first priority was to get back to Toronto to see my folks, who had been so very brave. I knew the loss of Evelyn had affected them deeply.

We cleared our travel plans at our Administration Office, and picked up travel warrants for Glasgow. Cam would do a side trip to Wolverhampton on the way up, to see his pilot's parents. There had been only two survivors in that crew. Both rear and mid upper gunners made it, although not without survivor's injuries. Two alive out of seven.

Cam got off at his junction for Wolverhampton, and I sat back, thankful for a seat all the way to Edinburgh. It was surprisingly quiet until the Polish Air Force started coming aboard. Out came the mickeys, and the conversation stepped up considerably. Most of them in this lot had married Scottish girls and were going home on leave. It had been four years since I had done that.

Every time I said, "Up the Polish Air Force," I got a free

drink. I was never going to make it to Edinburgh at this rate. I asked the one with the least perfume to hold my seat, and I regretted it the minute I said it. But, as it turned out, all was O.K. They just liked to smell nice, not to be nice.

There was a two hour lay over at Edinburgh, so I treated myself to a good supper nearby and sat at a window to watch the crowds on Princes Street. It certainly was busy. There weren't very many civilian cars, but there were trams galore, and thousands of people walking about. There was a radio playing near me, and I was pretty excited by what I heard. British forces were moving fast into Germany, with the Canadians leading the way to the north. Everyone I talked to was in an expectant mood.

I slept a part of the trip from Edinburgh to Glasgow. This was a good thing because it was a further ten miles to Uddingston by trolley car, and I still tired quickly.

As soon as I got on the trolley, I started looking for my old friends, but without success. At first I assumed they were not on duty, but then I remembered that it had been over two years since I last saw them. They might no longer have been with the company! There had been a lot of water under the bridge since then!

Never did a boy feel more at home than I did that day. Both Jeannie and Johnny were at home, and they gave me such a warm welcome. I dropped my kit in the hallway and headed straight to the kitchen stove and the tea pot. They both just laughed. First off, I told them that Cam would be along in a couple of days. They still looked on him as one of their own. Jeannie handed me a telegram addressed to me which read, "Mom and Dad rejoice in your safe return." That was enough for one day, so I excused myself and went to bed. For twelve hours I slept!

When I awakened, I wondered what part of heaven I was in. This little room was not only comfortable, but looked comfortable. That down comforter may have had something to do with it. The old fashioned pictures on the walls along with the bright coloured wallpaper also helped. For years I had had to live with wet cement block walls. And, for years before that, I had had to live with plain white plaster. No wonder I thought I was in heaven!

I washed and shaved, whistled and hummed, and then called

to Aunt Jeannie that I would be down in a minute. It was good to be alive.

My, breakfast was a fun time that day, and Johnny told me that Ian was due back any day now from his latest trip to India. So far, he had avoided torpedoes and again, according to Johnny, it was due to the speed his ship was able to reach. It was big and fast. Captain John was now a pilot on the Clyde, guiding all shipping into moorings. He had to know the tides along the length of this river. He no longer sailed the treacherous seas between Dublin and Glasgow, but had taken on an even more exacting position.

I phoned Scotty from Uddingston and left a message that I was in town, then I went for a walk to the grocery store with Aunt Jeannie. The streets were cobbled. It was such a strange surface to walk on. Once again, I had a formal introduction to the grocer. Jeannie was obviously well regarded in Uddingston and again the locals began to gather in the store. When I suggested to the owner he would have to expand, he just beamed. When he saw the ration card endorsed with "malnutrition," the gates opened wide. He just had to show the card to a couple of the locals. The noise level immediately went up two octaves. Since I figured this was the only hero treatment I could expect, I sopped it up like a sponge, and Jeannie and I giggled all the way home. I guess she knew the giggling was really due to a very healthy shot of scotch the grocer handed me in the back room. Best cure for malnutrition on the market!

When I arrived at the Locarno that evening, I found nothing had changed. This included the singer and the musical selection. The singer still didn't want to set the world on fire, and I would have assured her of this if she had only asked. There was excitement in the air, though. We all knew the war couldn't last much longer. Rumours were flying that Hitler had committed suicide, but no confirmation had been published as yet. It was time Turkey came into the war, though!

I danced with a couple of girls who seemed to be trying to assess the size of my wallet rather than staring at my handsome features. So, finally, I just sat down and ordered a drink and talked to myself. Fortunately, Scotty came along in the nick of time and changed all that. My, oh my, what a welcome, and on the dance floor too! We had a great deal to talk about. Cameron had arrived at Jeannie's and phoned Scotty's house to try to reach me. He wanted to stay at Jeannie's for the evening, which sounded sensible to me. It would have been a bit too much to go back into Glasgow right away.

While at the Locarno, I phoned Stan MacFarlane's house. His wife answered and told me they had been expecting my call. They had a party lined up for Thursday and wanted me to attend. I was pleased to accept. Bo would be there with bells on, she told me, and that I did believe.

When I returned to the table, some friends of Scotty's had moved in and were talking away to beat the band. I listened to the accent and thought, this sure is Glasgow! They had a tongue all their own. Scotty and I left early and walked home to her place. It was still so dark and grey, and left me feeling rather disappointed. Inside their flat, however, it was quite cheery. Scotty's mother was quiet and a little bit reserved, as I remembered her, but very kind. She welcomed me back, and invited Cam and me back for supper the next evening. We suggested that the date should include a bus trip out to Lock Lomond in the afternoon if Scotty's sister would join us, but that had to be put off until Sunday, since nobody just goofed off from the job during war years. Mrs. Thompson said Sunday would be all right for supper. I'm afraid working for a living had not entered my mind. I wasn't even sure I'd like it! Then I excused myself and headed back to Uddingston.

A pleasant reunion was in store for me since Ian was home. Jeannie and Captain John sat beaming at their errant boys, a group which, of course, included Cam.

Ian's lifestyle was so different from anybody I had ever known. It truly fascinated me. Here I had a full first cousin I had only met once before. On his return from India, he had become engaged to a girl in Liverpool, where his head office was located. Cam and I excused ourselves and went for a walk. The McCalls had had no time to themselves, and Ian was not staying over. It was a beautiful May night, so we didn't walk far but just sat on a stone fence and smoked while Cam told me about his visit to his dead pilot's parents. He had stayed over two nights with them. It was a brave thing for him to do.

Scotland is well to the north and, although the climate is tempered by warm tides, the skies above are very dark for long periods of time. This, in turn, is brightened by remarkable displays of Northern Lights. To sit and watch is quite a sight, one which we enjoyed that night.

When we returned to the cottage, Ian was just about to leave, so we wished the best to Captain Ian McCall and hoped his forthcoming marriage would be a success.

At breakfast the next morning, I explained to Jeannie that there was a crew get together that evening and she would have only one of her "boys" to feed. All her married life she had been used to the comings and goings of her men and accepted this fact readily. I left Uddingston about two o'clock in the afternoon for the MacFarlanes'. Beaupre was already there. Jenny MacFarlane was as beautiful as I remembered her. We ate snacks at the house and then went dancing. They even loaned me a girlfriend, which was very thoughtful, indeed. I was still on my feet at the bell, but getting a little amorous. She didn't mind a bit, and her friend in the Middle East wasn't objecting either. Besides, it was a necessity to stay over since I missed the last tram. She must have missed her bus, too.

Cam came in to town after breakfast, where we wanted to shop for a token gift for Jeannie. Scotty had suggested a silk scarf, but when the clerk said, "Aren't they beautiful? They come from India," that killed the idea right there. Ian had been on the India run for years and probably bought her dozens of them. I can't for the life of me remember what we did get for her.

That next day, Scotty and her sister, Mary, directed Cam and me to Loch Lomond, a fairly long tram ride. The last time I had been there was in 1941 when six of us, all from the same gunnery course in Mountainview, had travelled there on our first leave in Britain. John Castle and David Craig are the only names I remember. To the best of my knowledge, I'm the sole survivor of that group.

The weather wasn't quite with us, as usual, and we had a first-hand understanding now of the term "Scottish Mist." Wet fog would be a more apt name for it. We headed back to Scotty's flat.

This was, I think, the first time I had seen them all together at one time and this would be the last time. Although I dreaded telling Scotty I had decided to head home alone, as I felt more deeply for her than any girl to date, I guess home meant more. Here I was, twenty-four years of age and had never had a long, close association with any girl. I had been constantly on the move. We said good-bye on the stair at the doorway. Scotty knew instinctively I was leaving. The whole family was there, but Scotty said she loved me, and I told her the truth that I loved her, but would have to leave her behind. Let's face it, I felt terrible! I got no sympathy from Cam, either.

We decided to head back to Bournemouth and explained this to Aunt Jeannie. She was so very close to our hearts. We told her we were anxious, after all these years, to get back to Canada and our families. She understood completely and had been expecting this. We left the next day, which turned out to be a remarkable one in our lives. While in transit, the word spread that Germany had capitulated. The war in Europe was over.

Hitler had committed suicide in Berlin on April 30. Admiral Doenitz, who had been given control of all German forces at the last minute, put out peace feelers immediately. It was now the 4th day of May, 1945, and peace was arranged for Holland, Denmark, and north-west Germany. Unconditional surrender of all German forces on all fronts was to be effective on May 9.

Doenitz had tried to negotiate a favourable peace for the German people, but Eisenhower had said, "No. It must be total capitulation — and this is it!"

When our train pulled into London, it was like a zoo. I don't know who was minding the store because everyone was in the streets, all laughing and crying and shouting. It was truly amazing. Almost six years of pent up emotions released in four simple words.

"THE WAR IS OVER."

London had taken everything Hitler had to offer and never faltered. God bless them all!

It took us an hour to get the London-to-Bournemouth train. It seems everyone was on the move, and we spent half the time in the corridor for lack of setas, but it didn't matter much. It would have been far too noisy to sleep anyway, and it was a great deal more fun to join the crowd. One lady nearby was so excited because she could finally bring her children back home after years they had spent boarding on a farm away from the built up area. They had entirely missed a normal childhood because of the bombings.

There was mail waiting when we arrived at our billets. The biggest laugh of all was that our commissions had come through and were backdated for years. If the R.A.F. had notified us at the time, we would have had a few more comforts in the Officers' P.O.W. camp. Members of Canadian squadrons had been advised, and the proper German authorities were notified via the International Red Cross whenever there were changes in rank. These men were then moved to Sagan where most of the Allied Officers were held. Living conditions were better there — not much, but better.

We reported back to the Adjutant's Office about our latest uniform requirements and, once again, were given a clothing allowance and a travel warrant to London. This trip we delayed for a couple of days, to give ourselves a rest. This had been quite a ten day period. We had won the war single handedly and been promoted four ranks. We were now Flying Officers without ever having eaten a meal in an Officers' Mess!

Well, we finally did get back to London for new hats, shirts and arm band stripes. The stripes told people we were sprogs and, once again, we were very low on the totem pole. "Get some time in!" they shouted. We went for a lager at the Universal Brasserie and I wish to report that Trafalgar Square was still standing even after the severe beating it took on V.E. Day.

The Air Force interviewed me as to my intentions. My choice was to go home. The last time I had a choice, however, they sent me to Chatham, New Brunswick, so I suspected that my choice had nothing to do with their intentions. This time I really did have a choice, though, since all Aircrew in the R.C.A.F. had volunteered to fight in the European Theatre of War until the cessation of hostilities. We had now completed our contract, and we would be returning to Canada.

A bulletin informed us that ex-prisoners of war were given

194

the highest priorities for return to Canada, and all others would be required for policing for months to come. This bulletin then advised us to keep our Administration office notified as to our whereabouts. We would be heading out very soon for an embarkation port, and that was the word we were looking for!

- CHAPTER 25 -

We're Going Home

Since returning from Germany to Britain, one of the real treats had nothing to do with meals or pubs or girls. It was the "Public Caths." I found that to luxuriate in steaming hot water for a half hour, several times a week, beat everything. My afternoons were usually spent at the Pavilion watching the dancing and listening to the new Pilot Officers carrying out flying manoeuvres with their arms weaving above their drinks. The Bournemouth girls, unless they were very new here, had heard it all a hundred times before. But then again, that was the price of admission.

Someday soon, Bournemouth would revert back to the summer holiday and retirement town it had been before the war. All the wartime offices would close, and all those lovely girls who worked there would be gone. The Pavilion would be closed for months on end, but the gardens would continue until winter to attract thousands of people.

I phoned Uncle Jim's home in Sussex to tell them I was safely back in England, but could not take the time to visit because we had just received our embarkation warning, and we were standing by. They inquired about Glen McNicholl, and I told them the bad news. I could tell they had really liked Nic.

Finally, the word was posted. "Report to your Parade Square with your kit bag." They gave the specific time and day for embarkation. "We will proceed by rail to the embarkation point.

196

If your identification card and photo is not with you, you will not be allowed on board." That left us with two days in England to consume a few gallons of beer. What a way to go!

The ship we boarded was about three football fields long, and one Eiffel Tower high. The hammock space we were allocated was on "H" Deck, which was a long way down. The minute this tub was on the move, we decided to do something about that. In the meantime, hundreds of men refused to stay on board, and that tied things up beautifully until the dock master arrived and laid down the law. Evidently, the Dieppe P.O.W.'s figured they had had the slavery treatment long enough. They were not in the majority, however, otherwise, we might still be there. "Five days was all," they told us. Considering it had taken fifteen days on the water to get to England, this would be a fast trip. We tried to forget everything else, and remember we were going home! Well, at least Cam and I were in agreement on that one. There was something fiendishly funny about this, though. We had come over with first class accommodation, steward service and all. We were going home commissioned and sleeping in the hold. So hurrah for the Louis Pasteur, luxury liner.

Once we were moving, we took our hammocks down, packed them up, and picked up our kit bags. We climbed up to the main deck and, about mid way, unrolled our hammocks on the deck and took up squatters' rights. Nobody tried to move us. We were as happy as pigs in a wallow. No rain, please!

We were issued with life jackets and it was suggested that we wear them routinely. It was a terrific idea, and they made excellent pillows at night, too. There was the odd card game going on, and Cam and I were in and out of them, but nothing too heavy. For continuous action, however, the crap games took the show. Thousands of dollars were turning over every day. The Pay Officers would not allow anyone to take all his credits. They established a daily limit of five quid, and the rest went home.

After about three days of this, most of the boys were close to broke. The party atmosphere had settled down, except for the serious winners who huddled together in a small section of the room and rolled for the works. About ten men had all the money but, by the next morning, it would be down to two or three men.

197

Red Gordon from Brampton and Harrison from Calgary acted as policemen, good natured yet in control. Bill Pingle was on board with his big grin, along with Dabby Dabous, Brian Filliter and Stu Saunders. Dabby was putting on a last minute growing spurt, and soon would be able to see over the rail. Having had the same problem most of my life, I could appreciate his delight.

Boys from Sagan and from Penemunde were also on board. There were too many on board to spot everybody. I know George Harsh from Sagan was there, Wally Floody could not have been far behind, and Pop Kingdon and Walt Hoag must also have been there.

Everything was surprisingly quiet at the end of the trip. We were waiting to dock the next day at Halifax. It was cool on deck, but not cold. We had been lucky to travel at this time of year, otherwise we would have had to stay down under. There were a few dozen of us doing this sleeping on deck bit now. One thing about it, we woke up very early, and we were always first in for breakfast. Whether this was good or not, depended on the chef. He tried us sorely some days. We were not on a luxury liner anymore. We were back on rations, which still included lamb stew and those same old kippers for breakfast. Try that on a rough sea!

And then came the sound we all had been waiting for: "LAND AHEAD." What land it was, we didn't have the slightest idea, although we hoped we were close to Canada by now. Just imagine, I was still fifteen hundred miles from home! There was a time, though, when I was glad we lived a long way from the horrors of war and, thinking back, I can remember my Dad saying the very same thing.

When we finally got back to the docks, a real surprise awaited us. The Air Force Officer in charge of the Halifax area said we were not to disembark until the next day, and the war was on! To make matters worse, senior officers, squadron leaders and up were already heading down the runway. The ground swell of pent-up emotions was too great, and hundreds of men began pouring down the ramp. Most of these men had been away from home for many, many, years. No bureaucratic order would stop them now! Finally, they had to cordon off the dock area. Cam and I, at least, were finally off the ship.

198

Charlie at time of discharge

We sat on our kit bags for an hour or two, waiting for the word to come down. We would be given a meal in the assembly area, approximately one hundred yards down the road. We could sleep on board, if we wished, and we would load up for the trains at noon tomorrow.

Most of us decided to leave our kit at the assembly area and just sleep right there on the floor that night. Cam and I then headed into town. Although this was not our usual pattern, we stopped at a fruit store and bought a big bag of oranges, apples and bananas! Boy, what a treat! Since we would be on board the train for two days and nights, we stopped at the government store, where at least a thousand other servicemen were doing the same thing. Thank Goodness it wasn't Sunday!

There would be hundreds of our own boys getting off the train at each stop. Many of those, whose homes were in Nova Scotia, had already departed. Truro was next, and I couldn't help but think of Zeke Fox who would not be returning. In that sense, this was not a happy journey. These memories come flashing back, as did so many others. At Moncton, we dropped off many more, including Gummy MacDonald, McMurray, Brian Filleter, and Stu Saunders. These embarkations were not "official," as we were expected to report to Lachine on the way to Toronto for documentations. The Maritimers were not put on charge for it, however, since another riot would have been more than the politicians could stand.

By the time we got to Mount Joli, I was ready to admit that Canada was still a big, beautiful country, but, "Doesn't it come in a smaller size?" Then came Lachine, and we were exhausted.

It took two hours in long line ups to be documented and have travel warrants issued. Our departure was from old Bonaventure Station, where I felt quite at home. So much so that I fell asleep sitting on my dunnage bag. Cam jolted me out of that one.

At Toronto, Cam was being met at the station rather than the reception area in the "Horse Palace," so there was no need for us to go to the Exhibition grounds. Hundreds of people were waiting at the Union Station exit gates.

With the crowds behind me, I phoned home.

"Hello, Dad. I'm in Toronto. I'll be right home. Is Mom O.K.?"

Epilogue

I'm retired now and live at Sunnybrook Health Science Centre as an extended care resident. I have my freedom and my children have their sanity. How about that!

For over forty years, I travelled in sales. At first as a salesman, then as Sales Manager. For the past twenty years, I was a self-employed manufacturers' agent. My work took me across Canada many times and across the United States several times.

In 1946, I married a beautiful Toronto girl by the name of Leona (Lea) Gilham. We raised our daughter, Bonnie, and our son, Gordon. Bonnie (Wilson) is now a school teacher in Peterborough District and is married with two children. Gord is a Metro Police Staff Sergeant with a weird and wonderful career of his own. He has a lovely wife and two children.

We had lived in several cities in Ontario, as my job demanded, but we finally returned to Toronto in 1967 and settled in the Kingsway.

When Lea passed away in 1988, I tried living alone for three years. There was a limit to what my digestive system could take, then Chronic Respiratory problems set in requiring oxygen around the clock, so I moved to Sunnybrook. Fortunately, with the use of portable oxygen, I can get out for a few hours and am able to move around this huge complex with relative ease.

The support staff at Sunnybrook is truly remarkable. If a

veteran indicates an interest in a subject, he or she will promptly receive guidance if requested. When I first mentioned writing as a hobby, I was asked if I needed materials or assistance. At that time I had nothing as ambitious as a book in mind. The fact that a book did evolve is due to their encouragement.

The Red Cross ladies supply a large complement of volunteers at Sunnybrook. They take their jobs very seriously and go on shift each week as arranged. These are my "Lovely Ladies!" The creative arts section uses Red Cross ladies as well as their own skilled staff under the direction of Judy Mansell who, bless her soul, has arranged for some of my typing to be done by one of her instructors.

Recently, one of our most active volunteers at Sunnybrook was lost to cancer. Ever since his retirement, Mike Niewolski had combined his love for the caring for veterans through Red Cross participation at Sunnybrook. Lots of "Kriegies" do this. I see them pushing wheel chairs for the Red Cross every day. So much for retirement. I enjoy Bill Pingle, Al Wallace, and others, who drop in to see me during the week while they are making their rounds at the hospital. Bob Leavitt on Visitations is welcome any time.

When I was a boy, Catholics and Protestants rarely mixed. They were still fighting The Battle of the Boyne; the only things that had changed were the weapons. At the Orangemen's Parade in Toronto, they used to throw bottles of beer at each other. Today, things have settled down a bit. Now they drink the beer first.

Seriously though, Tony, our Sunnybrook priest, and Wayne, our Minister, are a large part of our life here. Both are a delight to know. Their support staff show up every Sunday. "Di" Pilkington and a lost sailor, by the name of Mac Upton, organize a team of wheel chair pushers and take patients to Sunday Services.

Nursing Directors may control the wards at our Veteran's Wing, but nurses run it! Our permanent staff are friendly and helpful. They go out of their way to make our life more comfortable. Barbara Paul is my primary nurse. She is all of the above, and let's face it, she's pretty too! What more can a man ask?

I can't thank one without thanking all!

My daughter Bonnie 1992

Let me tell you briefly about the ex-R.C.A.F. P.O.W. Association with members from every walk of life and from every part of the country. Each province has its own meeting place which is determined in advance, and you are welcomed with a "Royal Greeting" when you show up.

The Toronto group will have about twenty show up every Wednesday. Stu Saunders, my principal driver, will pick me up and deliver me to wherever the lunch is held.

Their wives must love this. They don't have to go — that's what they love!

Our Executive attends these lunches. Our National President, Don Morrison, plans nothing for the lunches, and, do you know, it works! There is much to do as Secretary, but Al Wallace doesn't let this worry us. He worries for us. He even tells us where next week's meeting will be. Howard (Howie) Copeman runs our National Publication, the "Camp," a very classy news magazine. It relies on our eight hundred remaining members to keep Howie up-to-date on our news. A list of some of these members that attend the luncheon follows.

After the Second World War, I was an active member in the Associated Canadian Travellers, a fraternal organization with seventeen branches in Ontario alone. When a salesman is moved to another city by his company, he immediately has friends and, more importantly, his wife meets the wives of other fellow travellers.

Some of my closest friends today are ACT members: Ralph Hutcheson; Gord Pammett, in Peterborough; George Dickinson and Bruce Griffiths, in London; Marv Hatelt, in Brampton; George Mountford, in Belleville; and Lorne Peebles, Lauren Simms and our secretary, "Sunshine," in Toronto.

It is a very long list. ACT has seven thousand members across Canada. Don't worry, I don't know them all!

My boyhood friends continued to prosper and are now retired.

Jack Alexander was on the management board of Toronto Hydro.

Hudson Mossop was a self-employed electrical Engineer and Consultant. His younger brother is a Judge in the Provincial Court system.

Doug Appleton will be retired now. He was a corporate Chartered Accountant, I believe.

John Slatter is a retired Department Head at C.I.B.C. and is a brother of Mary Johnson, who is so very active as a Sunnybrook volunteer with the Red Cross.

As to my air crew, Harold (Bo) Beaupre and I are in touch with each other regularly. He owned and operated a wholesale wall paper outlet for years. Now, rather than retiring, he is pursing his long-time stamp collecting hobby full-time and has a shop in an excellent location on the main street in Waterloo, Ontario.

George Bishop, who did his first tour with us, went on to do a second tour, but was shot down and taken prisoner. He was commissioned at the time and was sent to Sagan (the officers' camp). Bishop unfortunately died young after a very successful business career. His lovely wife and daughter live in the Toronto area.

Bo and I are the only Canadian survivors. Mac MacFarlane was in touch with us for a few years, but we have lost track of him. He was travelling internationally for his job and may have just found a better climate to live in.

Bill Lewis, who eventually replaced Bishop, was shot down with us, bailed out and was captured and sent to Sagan. Upon liberation, Bill transferred to the U.S. Army Air Force and took a D.F.C. and bar with him. After the war, he became a school teacher specializing in remedial work.

And finally, Cam. I figure the longer I can make him worry about what I might write, the better. Well, I have decided not to say anything. This way, he's sure to figure there must have been something wrong ... Actually, Cam has a lovely family and lives in Lorne Park, about twenty miles away. We make contact weekly. He is still one of my closest friends. I see him often with the "Lunch Bunch," our weekly ex-P.O.W. get-together, and our annual dances and barbecues.

Sunnybrooke Health Science Centre "Credits"

There are over 200 Red Cross volunteers that serve the veteran residents of the Kilgour and Hees Wings at Sunnybrook Health Science Centre. As a way of saying thank you for their help and friendship, I would like to mention a few I have gotten to know.

So, a big Thank You to:

Anita Hofstatter, Joyce Raper and the ladies and gentlemen of the Coffee Service.

Ilene Wonch and all her talented musicians.

Jessie Penny and the guys and gals of the Wheelchair Escort Service, especially: Paul Benson, Dorothy Copeman, Bill Graham, Mary Johnson, Mike Niewolski, Bill Pingle, Stu Saunders and Al Wallace and to Jan Suurmond and Tom Keating.

To the ladies of Market Place: Evelyn Davis, Doreen Fisher, Margaret Hogan, Grupta David, Wendy Maddock, Helen Robertson, Phyllis Waters, Jane Wiggins, Eileen Jeu, Betty Van and Pat Lawson.

And finally to staff person, Loraine Grant, who is the Volunteer Co-ordinator.

Sunnybrook Health Science Centre "Creative Arts Section"

An enjoyable part of my week is spent here. Judy Mansell, who manages this department, has gathered a clever group of artisans to teach any of us who want to learn. Judy herself is a clever worker and teacher.

My regular teachers, at present, are all highly skilled professional artists:

Lorrie Clarke	- Supervisor
John Andresen	- Instructor
Heather Bell	- Instructor
Susan Talamelli	- Instructor
Sandra McLean	- Volunteer Co-ordinator

and, a wonderful little lady volunteer named Jan.

There are many more teachers and various workshops covering Art, Painting on Silk, Woodwork, Ceramics, Leather work, Quilting, Plush Toys, etc.

POW — RCAF
Prisoner of War
Association's
"Lunch Bunch Attendees"

The following list, of course, represents the Association Members who reside in Central Ontario only who attend these informal luncheons held at various restaurants in Toronto, Ontario.

Don Morrision ✓	Mike Lewis	John Elliott
Stu Saunders	Dabby Dabous	Bill Pingle
Nick Carter	Bill Graham	Stan Croft
Bill Hennessey	Ed McCullough	Tass Kanakos
Don Elliott ✓	Don Morgan	Bruce Sutherland
Gillie Gillespie	Bob Alldrick	Ted Salmon
Doc Bullock	Jack Cameron	Frank Boyd
Mike Mackinnon	Howie Copeman	Harry Humphries
Tom Wiggins	Roy Hogan	Slim Chalmers
Ray Sherk	Al Wallace	Fred Stephens ✓
Ray Mountford	Earl Clare	Ed Horton
Grant Mcrae ✓	Peter Burnett	Joe McCarthy
Bill Charlesworth	Ross Gillespie	Peter Valachos
Glen Gardiner	Bob Madill	Don Lush
Bill Stephenson		

For more copies of

PAST TENSE — CHARLIE'S STORY

send $14.95 plus $3.00 for GST, shipping and handling to:
GENERAL STORE PUBLISHING HOUSE
1 Main Street, Burnstown, Ontario
Canada, K0J 1G0

Korea Volunteer	$17.95
Choco to A.I.F.	$14.95
Valour On Juno Beach	$14.95
Black Crosses Off My Wingtip	$14.95
The Ridge	$14.95
Trepid Aviator	$14.95
The Wing And The Arrow	$14.95
In The Line Of Duty	$39.95
Mud and Blood	$14.95
Ordinary Heroes	$14.95
One Of The Many	$14.95
Fifty Years After	$14.95
The Canadian Peacekeeper	$12.95
The Surly Bonds Of Earth	$12.95
The Memory Of All That	$14.95
No Time Off For Good Behaviour	$14.95
To The Green Fields Beyond	$14.95
Time Remembered	$14.95

For each copy include $3.00 to cover GST, shipping and handling.
Make cheque or money order payable to:

GENERAL STORE PUBLISHING HOUSE
1 Main Street, Burnstown, Ontario
Canada, K0J 1G0